"Dean Artenosi is the best in the Canadian real estate space! Why? Dean has seen it all, so he speaks from experience and knowledge. Brokerage owner, developer, land acquisitions, Dean has done it all in real estate, but what sets him apart is his passion and drive to share it with others."

—STACEY EVOY, president,
Ontario Real Estate Association 2022/2023

"Dean Artenosi has written a book that is essential to successfully navigating the world of real estate in Canada and the US today. You can feel his passion for this business jump out of every page and grab you. This memoir comes packed with thirty years' worth of experience told through stories: challenges, successes, lessons learned, heartbreaks, and triumphs. What you'll get from this book is mindset, vision, an unrelenting passion for doing the right thing for the customer, and suggested strategies on how to create wealth in real estate, all of which are critical in this business today."

—KARIM KENNEDY, CEO, Coldwell Banker Canada

"Dean Artenosi is a shining example of a successful entrepreneur. Follow the journey from salesperson to president, and learn how to do it for your clients, not to your clients! Dean's approach to his success has been through education—educating his clients and his salespeople to success. Dean spent his career making other people's lives better. Today, Dean, along with his wife Tania, own one of the largest real estate companies in Canada. This should be no surprise if you know Dean; you wouldn't expect anything less than number one. This book will outline his journey and his challenges, and you'll discover how to overcome the issues we all face. It's an inspirational read!"

—CHRIS LEADER, president, Leaders Edge Training

"Bold and real, Dean doesn't hold back in sharing thirty years of real estate wisdom, in easy-to-act mindset pillars and action steps. It's a people business; serve your clients' needs, build relationships that last, and that in turn builds wild success and real wealth. I love the way Dean cuts through everything to hammer this point home (and many other significant insights) and tell you exactly how to do it yourself while sharing his incredible story of ups and downs that delivered his lessons."

—VONNY FAST, Hall of Famer #1 Rep in Canada, Cutco

"It takes time and patience to grow a tree. This is not a book for anyone looking to get into real estate for a quick win. That's not what long-term success is all about. It's about day-in, day-out, having the right mentality, and doing what's right."

—BILL ARMSTRONG, general manager, Arizona Coyotes

"Dean Artenosi has written a must-read primer for anyone wanting to understand and learn about real estate. Read this book and learn from one of the best. Good leaders provide direction, purpose, and reason for a group or organization to follow. They also share their knowledge, wisdom, and experience with others. Their leadership becomes a calling to serve others. Dean Artenosi is a leader who has risen to their position in their company and industry through his actions and words. His thoughts on real estate in every aspect of it are clear, specific, and on target in today's business and social climate."

—LISA PATEL, Property Princess Inc.;
former president, TRREB Toronto Regional Real Estate Board;
director, Large Ontario Real Estate Association

ONWARDS AND UPWARDS

ONWARDS

AND

UPWARDS

DISCOVER THE REALITY OF
BUILDING REAL ESTATE SUCCESS

DEAN ARTENOSI

Forbes | Books

Published by Forbes Books, Charleston, South Carolina.
Member of Advantage Media.

Forbes Books is a registered trademark, and the Forbes Books colophon is a trademark of Forbes Media, LLC.

Printed in the United States of America.

10 9 8 7 6 5 4 3 2 1

ISBN: 979-8-88750-036-2 (Hardcover)
ISBN: 979-8-88750-037-9 (eBook)

Library of Congress Control Number: 2023909663

Cover design by Analisa Smith.
Layout design by Lance Buckley.

This custom publication is intended to provide accurate information and the opinions of the author in regard to the subject matter covered. It is sold with the understanding that the publisher, Forbes Books, is not engaged in rendering legal, financial, or professional services of any kind. If legal advice or other expert assistance is required, the reader is advised to seek the services of a competent professional.

Since 1917, Forbes has remained steadfast in its mission to serve as the defining voice of entrepreneurial capitalism. Forbes Books, launched in 2016 through a partnership with Advantage Media, furthers that aim by helping business and thought leaders bring their stories, passion, and knowledge to the forefront in custom books. Opinions expressed by Forbes Books authors are their own. To be considered for publication, please visit **books.Forbes.com**.

To all the aspiring real estate agents and entrepreneurs throughout the world.

CONTENTS

THE REAL WORLD OF REAL ESTATE

I hate to open with an unsettling newsflash, but you're being misled about the inner workings of the real estate world.

I don't know what better way to drive this point home than to blare it loudly and clearly right from the jump—and then hammer it home with great force, the way you'd stake a For Sale sign deep into a soft patch of grass.

Ignore the buzzwords of the moment. Drone out the glorified carnival barkers who insist that success in the real estate business requires building smooth "downlines" and navigating needlessly complex "multilevel marketing schemes."

Don't be fooled by the snooty arrogance of brands that tout their "national reach." Ignore the folks that blather on about their oversized "market share."

It's pure nonsense. All real estate agents have the same market share because we all have the same exposure to properties through the multiple listing service (MLS) system.

Here's the key takeaway that every real estate developer, agent, and investor needs to remember: this is—and always will be—a *people* business. Clients. Partners. Coworkers. Investors. Brokers.

Ultimately, it's the quality of the connections that you make—and the lengths that you go to preserve and strengthen them—that will be your greatest differentiator.

All that other stuff is just white noise and siren songs dreamed up by people who are driven more by ego and self-aggrandizement than a sense of genuine purpose.

You don't need any of that hokum to find success in the real estate world. Don't believe a single syllable of it, because no one enters our business hoping to become a glorified Amway rep.

If I may be so bold as to give it to you straight without the thousand red balloons and piped-in applause. I've built one of the most successful real estate practices in Ontario, Canada—and generated *real* wealth—by remaining laser focused on listening to and addressing the needs of my clients. *Period. Full stop.*

Mindsets and skill sets matter too, as does an ability to devise creative financing solutions. But if you can stay grounded and humble and remain open to learning, you will prevent yourself from becoming a prima donna.

Clients will work with you because they trust *you*. Because they appreciate the rapport you've built with them. And, most importantly, because you've provided them with a level of service that they won't be able to find anywhere else. That's real advice. And that's what the real estate industry—and this book—is all about.

I view myself, essentially, as a problem solver. I am not a life coach. I can't help you work through marital issues. Or offer salient advice on how to ensure your child gains acceptance into their elite university of choice. But I have devoted my professional life to helping people make prudent decisions about real estate.

If you're seeking anything that includes the words "get rich quick" or "scheme," I'll save you the suspense. It's not in here. This is a book built around a very specific catalog of wisdom, which I've accumulated over the last thirty years.

In the following pages, I'm open sourcing it and giving it away for everyone to use as they see fit.

I've decided, at long last, to actually put a pen to paper because I've been around long enough to have peeked behind the proverbial curtain. I know what works and what doesn't.

I can identify the real empire builders from the real estate agents who are all glitter and no substance. This book is designed to ensure you become the former and avoid devolving into the latter.

So I'll keep things as simple and practical as I can. Interested in learning the best way to devise truly creative financing vehicles? How to properly assemble a portfolio? The ways to assess the value of a piece of land? Why the vast majority of great properties are on corner lots? Or why there's more value to be found in buying existing properties rather than investing in new construction?

Then, by all means, read on. It's all here for you in good, old-fashioned black and white. I've also endeavored to make these lessons as jargon-free as possible because I've found that simple language has the longest shelf life.

But at the end of the day, these tips and strategies are really just a means to a greater end. My core philosophy remains the same today as it was on day one: success is a natural byproduct of providing unparalleled service to clients.

So that's my lead-in—the first truism worth highlighting in bright yellow marker: *make it about them, not you.* Help others solve their problems and build equity, and your good works will boomerang back to you tenfold, providing you opportunities to develop a stronger business and generate untold wealth for yourself.

For years I've politely listened to real estate cheerleaders insist that they've devised a panacea—fail-safe formulas that will guarantee novice real estate agents and investors instant success.

"Just pour, stir, and mix it all together," they say, "and, voilà! Instant money-making powers will be yours!"

I offer you no such guarantee. There's no snake oil being hawked here. Quite the contrary, I'd argue that the chorus of contemporary voices who are obsessed with "branding" and "multilevel marketing" have things backward.

If I were to draw a pie chart that captures what is required to enjoy long-term success in our business, I'd carve out a segment for branding that represents no more than 5 percent of the whole pie.

I can say this with unwavering confidence because I've been in this business since I was in my midtwenties. I was born into a family of Realtors. Both sides of my family were Italian immigrants who used real estate to lift themselves out of poverty in Ontario.

Multiple branches of my family tree have been carved with names of people who were born to buy and sell land. My father devoted his life to this business, as did my entire family.

Look at the top branches of that same family tree and you'll see that my wife, Tania, works in this field too. She has not only established her own glimmering reputation but has also been instrumental in helping me run our real estate brokerage: The Real Estate Centre, which is commonly referred to as TREC, under the Coldwell Banker umbrella.

In this book I've carefully assembled a collection of stories that will help you navigate your way through a whole host of challenges.

I recognize that time is a precious commodity, so they're relatively short parables. Each is meant to illustrate a set of core tenets that are rarely offered on the real estate lecture circuit these days.

Some stories offer practical and actionable pieces of advice that you can tuck into your memory bank (or briefcase) and use as needed. But others, admittedly, are more philosophical in nature. Some are rooted in my admiration for the new urbanism movement, which seeks to revitalize existing communities and curb the expansion into our precious open spaces and natural green fields.

Let me also stress one point: given the circuitous route I took to find my true calling, I recognize the benefits that this profession can bestow. I firmly believe that working in the real estate industry can—and often does—change the trajectory of people's lives, not just financially but emotionally and psychologically as well.

It certainly changed mine. As a young man, I carried around big heaping fistfuls of anger and resentment, much of it the result of my challenging upbringing. As in so many homes, a divorce split my family apart when I was young. Battle lines were drawn, leaving me suspended in an uncomfortable limbo between two warring factions.

This business helped me channel all my pent-up anger and use it to burn through some of those early insecurities. I sincerely believe it can do the same for you, no matter how many obstacles may currently lie in your path. Real estate allowed me to actualize my talents, which were obvious to others but often lay fallow in me.

I hope this book will gently nudge you in a similar direction and help you find your own definition of fulfillment and personal enrichment.

This book is my personal road map, the first step in a continuing journey that requires you to believe that both change and success are, indeed, possible.

But as we all know, optimism alone will never suffice. We all need mentors, in some form or another.

It's my hope that I can serve as a trusted mentor by dispensing some of the hard-earned wisdom I've acquired while building my business and—more importantly—improving its stature.

In the end there's one common denominator that's shared by virtually everyone who's enjoyed long-term success in our field. And that lodestar is the right *mindset*.

Optimism alone will never suffice.

Cultivate the wrong one during any phase of your career—especially at the beginning—and you're essentially moonwalking in the wrong direction.

I can't stress this point enough: there's no single prescription that will yield success. You can't pop two pills—or absorb two pithy talking points—and suddenly wake up the next morning a real estate mogul. It takes work—a lot of hard work—but it also helps to have the right mindset in place to set that winning process in motion.

In fact there's a pretty clear order of operations that will dramatically increase your chances of success. First, you have to cultivate the right mindset, which acts as a kind of X-ray vision that enables you to view properties, homes, and parcels of land in ways that others can't see them. Then, and only then, can you progress onward to the next stage and develop the skill sets required to execute on that initial vision.

So let's start right there. Ask yourself this question: Which mindset would you prefer to adopt—a feudal one that incentivizes you to serve the interests of others or an entrepreneurial one that will differentiate you from the competition?

Take it from someone who toiled away at an eclectic mishmash of different jobs when I was a young man: it's never too late to change your mindset and make the turn. Just look at my early resume for evidence of that fact. At one point or another, I've sold Cutco knives. I ran a carpet-cleaning service. I shoveled snow. I developed an eco-friendly cleaning product. I even, during a particularly lean stretch, sold boxes of garbage bags.

But here's the upshot of all those early career choices: they each prepared me, in their own unique way, for the success I'd eventually find in real estate.

I wouldn't trade, for instance, the tutelage I received from two of my sales mentors, Adam Ginsberg and Joe Grushkin, while I was selling Cutco knives for anything in the world. They helped mold and shape me into the real estate entrepreneur I am today.

I'll never forget the energy Joe used to bring to his meetings and motivational sales meetings. He'd literally sprint up to the podium and unleash a palpable wave of energy out into the crowd. At the end of his presentations, I'd always leave the room fired up and ready to accept the next challenge. But what I loved the most was the way he closed every speech. He'd say the same thing every time he left the dais. "Onward and upward," he'd yell. And we'd all walk out of the room feeling as if we could do anything, as if someone had blasted us right out of the mouth of the cannon, flying skyward, above the clouds.

It reminded me, in all honesty, of something my aunt Anna used to always say. I would ask her, "*Zia Anna, come stai?*" meaning, "How are you?" Her response to me would always be "*Sempre tiranti avanti,*" which translates to "Always moving forward."

I want you to feel that sense of freedom and confidence—of moving forward, of ascending onward and upward—at the close of this book.

Because chances are you've likely traversed a strange and winding career path yourself—one that's every bit as curvy and uncertain as mine was in my twenties. But I guarantee you this: all those stops along the way weren't for naught. They can be used to your advantage in the real estate world.

After all there's no school or degree or workshop that can ever completely prepare you for this kind of work. It's more like speeding across a multilane expressway crisscrossed with innumerable on- and off-ramps. The key is to make a commitment to this crazy-beautiful world we call the real estate industry—and just turn the wheel. Make that turn.

I'd argue there's no better time to do that than the present. But that's your call. If you're holding this book, chances are your turn signal is already flashing. Maybe you're sitting, idled, in what feels like a career traffic jam. Perhaps that professional pileup is stunting your true potential.

My advice: make the turn. Make it by turning the page and reading on. After all, we have a whole lot of real estate to cover in the pages to follow ...

THE PARABLE OF GEORGIAN BAY:

CULTIVATING A REAL ESTATE MINDSET

My real estate journey began with a bang so jarring you could hear it from one end of Ontario, Canada, to the other. It wasn't a particularly pleasant sound. Not the thrilling thunder of a fireworks extravaganza. Nor the triumphant cannon fire that marks Tchaikovsky's 1812 Overture.

Quite the opposite. It was more of a deafening pop, followed by a slow fizzle. This was back in 1990, fresh on the heels of a decade-long rise in the value of Toronto real estate.

Equities? Who needed them? Real estate investments had been on an absolute tear; they seemed to be a one-way escalator that only climbed upward.

And then, quicker than you can say "earnest money," came the aforementioned pop.

One of the most massive real estate bubbles in Canadian and North American history had officially gone kaput. It was a sudden and painful drop, followed by a slow, wheezy deflation that quickly flattened asset prices, then squeezed them even lower for years thereafter.

Homes. Buildings. Commercial properties. Land. Everything fell.

Dollars degraded, virtually overnight, into quarters, dimes, and nickels, including the value of a property that had special significance to my family: a pristine fifty-acre parcel of land on Georgian Bay, Ontario, about an hour's drive north of Toronto.

I was in my twenties at the time, still sharpening my entrepreneurial skills by selling Cutco knives door to door. The 1990 downturn hit me hard—not so much professionally as personally, as a number of members of my family had invested in buying that parcel of land on Georgian Bay.

Although virtually everyone felt the ill effects of the Great Real Estate Cataclysm of 1990, we felt it more acutely than most. In fact it's not hyperbole to say that the downturn quite literally ripped my family apart.

My father had purchased the aforementioned land on Georgian Bay a few years earlier for $600,000. With the market running hot, he did what any experienced real estate developer would've done: he packaged the land up and flipped it, selling it to a group of investors for a total of $1.2 million.

It just so happened that both sides of my family had rushed and signed up to be members of that consortium of buyers.

The timing of that purchase, for them, proved suboptimal. With real estate prices soaring, a psychology of irrational exuberance had set in. And much like the dot-com bubble before it, what had leaped skyward was about to come crashing down to earth.

Timing is everything, isn't it?—in both real estate and life. And thus when the trap door slid open, it sent the value of the Georgian Bay property spiraling straight into an abyss.

Why, you might be wondering, are we starting our discussion about real estate with the story of a heartbreaking downturn, one of the most disturbing periods in recent memory?

Answer: this is a book about the *real* world of real estate.

It bothers me to see so many young real estate agents and investors being spoon-fed half-truths and told deceptive fairy tales about the way our business works.

I want this book to be grounded in reality. To be more raw and more honest about what's actually required to build substantial wealth in our industry.

If you can endure difficult times and emerge from them stronger than you were during good times, you're more than halfway to your goal.

I see myself as a problem solver. And I hope you will too, because that's what you'll need to be—month in and month out, year after year—when working with real estate.

Anyone can do well when they're working with a dream client or during boom times, but you really separate the wheat from the chaff when you suddenly find yourself staring at a brick wall when you expected nothing but open roads ahead of you.

Don't expect a smooth ride. Problems will, undoubtedly, envelope you: Problems with your business. Problems with your developments. And problems that your clients will unexpectedly toss into your lap.

That is why it's critical for you to develop a very specific kind of mindset. I'd argue that this mindset consists of a series of pillars—think of them as a set of indestructible bearing beams. If you can understand and internalize these pillars, your chances of success will increase exponentially.

> **Don't expect a smooth ride. Problems will, undoubtedly, envelope you.**

Pillar No. 1: To be successful in the real estate business, you should view yourself, first and foremost, as a problem solver.

And it's safe to say that, in 1990, I had problems galore.

My parents divorced when I was a young man. Their split opened up deep wounds and anger in me, which I carried into adulthood. I'd come to grips with the fact that my parents had not been, to put it mildly, a compatible match. It would've been hell on earth for either of them to remain married to the other, but the great crash of 1990 exacerbated my insecurities.

At the time everyone, on every branch of my family tree, seemed to be lawyering up over the purchase of that parcel of land on Georgian Bay. It was a Capulets-versus-Montagues kind of mentality. On one side: members of both my mother's and father's families. And on the other: my father.

I found myself caught in the middle but remained sympathetic to my father's position. He insisted, time and again, that he'd done absolutely nothing wrong.

And for the most part, I agreed with him.

The price of land can go up. And the price of land can go down. Every real estate investor, my father insisted, should understand that most basic of truths. It just so happened that after my father sold his Georgian Bay property to a group of investors that he assembled, the market crashed.

These were forces at work that were beyond his control. Why couldn't his family, he insisted, face that inconvenient truth?

This brings us to **Pillar No. 2: Real estate is an industry rife with—and driven by—emotions.** This is an irrefutable fact. It isn't all rose gardens and four-car garages. It would be nice if the real estate world was driven by reason and logic, but more times than not, it's driven by our emotions, by a deep and abiding fear that we're going to miss out on the opportunity of a lifetime.

If you're one of those fortunate few who possess true emotional intelligence, make sure to lean into that superpower, because it will rarely lead you astray.

One of the questions to ask yourself, especially when it comes to real estate, is this: Can you govern your emotions while assessing the emotional states of others?

Because that's a critical component of a real estate mogul's mindset. Sometimes, buying and selling and renovating can be exhilarating work. Sometimes, it can be scary. Sometimes, things can turn ugly. And sometimes, it can feel like you're right smack in the middle of a winner-take-all war.

In regard to the dispute over Georgian Bay, I found myself squarely in the latter category.

Let it be said that success in real estate requires a fertile imagination. It doesn't matter what type of project you're pursuing. A picturesque plot of oceanfront land. A hard-luck neighborhood. A run-down old house that's seen far better days. Or a high-tech warehouse sitting on an expansive suburban lot.

If you can look at any sliver of land and see a potential future—in crystal-clear four-K resolution—that doesn't yet exist but could materialize over time, I can teach you pretty much everything else you need to learn.

That's **Pillar No. 3: Real estate requires both vision and an entrepreneur's mindset.**

Your imagination should operate like a time-lapse camera. It should be able to fast-forward through weeks, months, and years and see what a parcel of land could become over time rather than what it currently looks like in the present moment.

We all must ask ourselves those two basic questions over and over again: What does the property in question currently offer? And what can I envision it offering in the future?

Those are the two poles, with a huge spectrum of options in between. So start with your end vision and work backward from there.

Which brings us back to Georgian Bay in the late 1980s and early 1990s. What exactly did my father and others see in this place to compel them to pour their hard-earned capital into it?

What, in other words, was so special about Georgian Bay?

Back in the late 1980s, most people would have said, "Not much."

Was it a picturesque spot? Without a doubt. The area was, and remains, a hiker's paradise. It boasts a perfect trifecta of natural wonders—lush forests, granite coastlines, and pristine waterways— plus the added benefit of candy-cane-colored lighthouses speckled across its beautiful coastline.

Nevertheless, moneyed Toronto families interested in buying or building idyllic waterfront retreats invariably looked farther east to build their second and third homes. They always circled the same spots on their atlases: the gorgeous Muskoka district, located roughly two hours north of Toronto.

Muskoka was and remains an idyllic vacation destination. It's cottage country, Canada's answer to the Lake District in northern England. Once a hub for the lumber trade, in Muskoka clouds of sawdust had given way to lush areas marked by stunning foliage, sunset cocktail cruises, and pockets of gorgeous homes.

Whenever a Muskoka house hit the market, it was gobbled up immediately. Affluent families passed down their boathouses and grand mansions, generation after generation, to their children and grandchildren.

Even back in the 1980s, there was an undeniable cachet to the place. If you set down secondary roots in Muskoka, your social credit score rose immediately. As such it was a place that proved particularly attractive to the nouveau rich, as they attempted to rise up the ranks in the go-go 1980s.

So what exactly did Georgian Bay have to offer that Muskoka didn't? Well, for one, it had large tracts of undeveloped and sparsely populated land. It was precisely the kind of place, my dad surmised, that could be converted into a waterfront resort without negatively impacting the natural environment.

Whenever he drove north, he could envision a glorious future. Measuring 120 miles long and 50 miles wide, Georgian Bay felt like a giant infinity pool waiting to be claimed. A chain of rivers—the French, the Muskoka, the Severn—poured into the bay, creating deep, pristine blue waters fringed by lush forests and the occasional apple grove.

It was easily accessible too. You could cruise up to Georgian Bay from Toronto in half the time it took you to reach Muskoka. The shorter the drive, the fewer times little Jimmy and Susie would be compelled to ask, "Are we there yet, Mom and Dad? Are we there yet?"

Plus there were plenty of diversions encircling Georgian Bay to keep everyone happy. There were national parks and state parks in the vicinity. Drive ten minutes one way and you'd find yourself on a ski hill. Travel twenty minutes in the other direction and you could hit the blackjack tables and give the roulette wheel a spin at an area casino. Most important of all, the parcel that my dad had assembled included seven hundred glorious feet of easily accessible beachfront land.

So the big difference between these two gorgeous pieces of land came down to this fact: Muskoka was move-in ready. Its reputation had already been established years ago. You didn't have to use your imagination when you bought into Muskoka, because it was already a well-established, turnkey paradise.

But Georgian Bay was all raw potential. At the time, a relatively modest number of people were enjoying that side of the bay. But whenever my dad drove up there, he'd stand on that immaculate shoreline and feel the stillness and solitude ripple right through him.

Here, he surmised, was a real-deal, once-in-a-lifetime real estate opportunity.

So my father took the plunge. He invested in the promise of the place knowing that it would take time—a very long time—to reach its full potential.

Which leads me directly to **Pillar No. 4: In the real estate world, time is both a precious short-term commodity and a long-term asset.**

In the immediate term, you have to act quickly. In a bull market like the one that fueled the 1980s real estate boom, you can't dillydally. You either move on an idea or abandon it. It's pretty much a binary decision.

My dad of course acted on his instincts. He purchased his fifty-acre parcel on Georgian Bay, which included a single cottage located a stone's throw away from the shoreline.

His vision, from the very beginning, was to sell that parcel back to a group of investors. He'd then use that additional influx of capital to improve the land and help develop the area in a responsible way.

Given the overheating market, he was overwhelmed with interest. All in all it took him just six months to assemble a group of investors—which included people from both sides of my family—and sell the parcel to that consortium for $1.2 million.

This is a fancy way of reminding you that real estate is, by nature, a speculative asset.

When you purchase land, you have to accept the risks that come along with that investment. I can't stress this point enough, especially for those of you who are new to our industry. Just because you can visualize a glorious future for a property does not guarantee you that (a) it will ever come to fruition or (b) it will develop according to your own timeline.

Real estate investments do not follow a linear path. In most cases you have to lumber your way, zigzagging back and forth and up and down, to the finish line—leaping over all manner of unexpected hurdles along the way.

From my father's perspective, everyone was running a marathon, not a hundred-meter dash. He'd already run the first leg of the race by risking $600,000 of his own money to buy the property. Then, he did what real estate investors often do: he sold his property when prices were high to earn a profit on the risk he'd taken.

By contrast my family and the other investors felt like they were investing in a sure thing, not realizing that sometimes the real estate market can spin out into a sudden and unforeseen nosedive.

So after the zeppelin-sized real estate bubble burst in 1990, my family became more and more apoplectic with anger over the purchase of this dream property on Georgian Bay.

I know, because I personally witnessed all the threats and lawsuits they lobbed at my father throughout the ensuing decade.

As the real estate market remained depressed, my father recognized that the only prudent decision was to wait things out. He is, after all, a real estate developer. Pretty much every new deal completed in 1989 had lost money. Why, he asked his family, did they expect him to bail them out when the entire market was in the tank?

On the one hand, I empathized with his predicament. Regardless of the hurt I'd experienced when my parents divorced, I idolized my father. He was—and remains—the smartest man I've ever known. His IQ and real estate acumen are both off the proverbial charts.

When I was younger, he used to drill in me one particularly sage piece of advice. Let's call it **Pillar No. 5: Your end goal when investing in real estate should be to build long-term wealth.** And *true* wealth creation, he always added, requires a long-term time horizon.

Turns out he was 100 percent correct. Crossing the *real* finish line, not the arbitrary checkpoints along the way, requires fortitude, character, and a somewhat steely-eyed nature. In short, you need imagination to succeed, but you need perseverance and execution to win in the end.

I never thought I'd follow in his footsteps until the mid-1990s, after years spent in sales and running my own company. When I decided to make my transition into the real estate world, my father didn't give me a dime, nor did I work for him directly.

He wanted me to pave my own way, which I did by taking a rather unconventional path.

Early in my career, I'd showed a talent for helping buyers, rather than sellers. And along the way, I pioneered some rather unorthodox marketing strategies.

Truth be told I entered the real estate scene at the right time. Prior to 1995, real estate agents and Realtors could only represent sellers, because it was the seller who paid the commission. As you might imagine, this produced a far more cutthroat industry than you'll find today, especially in and around Toronto.

Competition, in the old days, was fierce because there was a limited pool of sellers and a lot of real estate agents and Realtors jockeying for their business.

A change in real estate regulations in 1995 allowed us to represent buyers for the first time. For an ambitious young upstart real estate man like me, this was nothing less than a blessing from the property gods.

I was determined, even back then, to become more than just a real estate agent. My father had given me some sound advice, which I took to heart: **Pillar No. 6: "You create wealth in real estate by building and managing a strong portfolio of assets, not by chasing leads."**

And although I was still green, I was beginning to understand the wisdom of those words. I certainly wanted to generate substantial wealth. Who doesn't, right? But I also felt a responsibility to help renters become property owners.

If you've ever spent so much as a day in Toronto, you know it's a beautiful smorgasbord of all different kinds of people, ethnicities, religions, and cultures. I love Toronto. And given all the stories I'd heard as a child from my father about the struggles he experienced being the sole Italian immigrant in his neighborhood, I felt that this was my way of paying our good fortune forward.

If my goal was to amass wealth, what better way to do so, I concluded, than by helping renters become homeowners?

Early in my career, I ran a rather unconventional marketing campaign. I designed, wrote, and placed ads in the classified sections of local newspapers. Although they weren't works of art, they were built around a novel financing strategy—I called it my "lease-to-own, no-money-down" contracts—that proved extraordinarily appealing to people.

It was a completely unorthodox idea at the time. But people were drawn to it like iron filings to a magnet. No sooner did I begin to place ads in local papers than I was inundated with phone calls. This influx of interest drew the ire of established players, some of whom did everything in their power to try and muscle me out of the business before I could gain a foothold.

During those early years, I went to war with a lot of jealous rivals. One Realtor in particular tried to spoil my reputation and run me out of the industry by asking the Real Estate Council of Ontario to bar me for running what he called "unethical" ads.

It didn't work. There was nothing remotely illegal or unethical about those ads. If anything, my "no-money-down" contracts were a godsend to low- and middle-income borrowers. And in short order, my ads proved so alluring that others in the industry began copying me, often placing their ads right next to mine.

By the mid-1990s, I owned roughly twenty properties, many in a hardscrabble area of the greater Toronto area in Newmarket nicknamed the "Dogpatch." I felt I'd found a higher purpose. I was helping renters become homeowners, which helped heal some of the wounds I'd carried with me due to the internal squabbles between my father and other members of my family.

As I tell every up-and-coming Realtor who needs advice, there is a preferential order of operations in our line of work. The more successful you are in representing buyers, the more quickly you'll find success as a real estate investor. Time spent helping others will improve the probability that you will help yourself.

And that brings us to **Pillar No. 7: Long-term success in the real estate market is a byproduct of building a strong portfolio of real estate properties and then being patient enough to play the long game.**

What disappointed me more than anything about my family's reaction to the Georgian Bay situation was their stubborn unwillingness to admit that the real estate market will invariably experience peaks and valleys. There will be shifting real estate cycles just as sure as there will be wintertime snow in Canada.

Real estate prices will go up. Real estate prices will go down. Sometimes, you'll be caught in an updraft or pulled back down during a recession. The fact of the matter is that no one ever wants to think things can go wrong until they do.

My advice about uncertain real estate markets comes down to this: you have to muster up the willpower and the character to stick things out. Keep your wits about you when everyone else seems to be losing theirs, and you'll likely win out in the end.

> **You have to muster up the willpower and the character to stick things out.**

I can recall, during the late 1990s, sitting in a boardroom with my father during contentious negotiations over the fate of the Georgian Bay property. I sat on one side of the table with my father and his lawyer. And on the other side sat a legion of people from his own bloodline—his nephew and the spouses of his nieces, their families, and others.

Emotions ran high. No one was going to back down from this particular fight. My family demanded that my dad take a loss and buy them out. My father, who is as stubborn as any man in this world, shot icy glares across the table and said, "No way in hell. You bought the land. The market crashed. Deal with it."

Looking back I understand his point now more than ever. There's no sure thing in real estate. Money will come in and go out, sure as the tides at Georgian Bay. And in most cases, large swaths of your savings will be tied up in land and properties.

This is an extremely important point for aspiring real estate agents and real estate investors to recognize. Since so much of your capital is not liquid, you're unlikely to have as much cash in the bank as your neighbors.

You will be tied down more, financially speaking, than they will. You will own a parcel of land that you're going to have to continually sink money into. The key, I've found, is not to view those payments as money wasted but rather as the table stakes required to experience a much larger payout down the line.

A life spent in real estate does demand sacrifices. Perhaps your investments will prevent you from buying that new car you really want. They might, on occasion, prevent you from sending your kids to that premiere hockey camp that they begged to attend. But that's part and parcel of the deal. True real estate investors recognize that these commitments are essential to executing their long-term plan and winning in the long run.

As the litigation and the recriminations between my father and my family continued to rage in the late 1990s, I'd regularly drive up to Georgian Bay, drink up the gorgeous landscape, and recognize the true potential of the place.

Times were tough. A resort concept in nearby Victoria Harbor had slid into receivership. Many people's dreams had been broken, and some checkbooks had been drained. But I firmly believed that, over time, this gorgeous stretch of Canada would come roaring back to life.

I was in my midtwenties at the time, still caught in the crossfire of my family's escalating civil war. "Perhaps," I told myself, "I can play referee here. Maybe this is a problem I can help solve."

I hatched a plan. What if I took some of the proceeds from real estate investments and began purchasing parcels surrounding the fifty acres in Georgian Bay?

By swooping in and buying that land at depressed prices, I would be able to average down the losses of that original parcel on Georgian Bay. As any real estate developer knows, averaging down on land is akin to a stock investor buying more shares of a trusted company at depressed prices.

My goal was to build a larger stake in this beautiful stretch of land on Georgian Bay, while simultaneously brokering a ceasefire to the hostilities within my own family.

So I started buying additional parcels in Georgian Bay. Some were small, just 30 acres in size; others were as expansive as 120 acres.

When I surveyed the land, I noticed an abandoned old railway line that cut right through a huge swath of the area. To my mind those lines created a natural severance in the property. By acquiring land on both sides of the split, I was buying one parcel that I could divide into two.

When I walked those railroad tracks, I didn't see rails and nails. I saw future walking trails and bike paths, all paved with spongy cement, which could be repurposed for the betterment of future residents and the land itself.

I saw a future filled with people canoeing and biking and roller-blading—activities that promoted good health while still preserving the natural beauty of the area. I envisioned a sixteen-kilometer-long trail connecting various townships, complete with signage and rest stations dotting the way.

I looked into securing private mortgages and then traveled the area asking current owners if they had any interest in selling their land.

Pillar No. 8: Real estate is—and will always remain—a "people business." It doesn't matter what bright, shiny new technology debuts next week, the process invariably ends by siting down, one on one, with someone in their living room and talking to them.

My heartfelt advice: listen more, talk less. But above all be genuine. Be low-key, not flashy. Humble not egotistical. Build a rapport with people, and you'll be surprised at how much you can actually achieve.

Throughout the late 1990s, I'd sit down with landowners of adjoining land and build a strong enough and genuine rapport with them that they wanted me to own their property as they felt good about who I was and my humble approach. If they agreed to sell, I'd always pay them a fair market price for their land. They were more than happy to sign on the dotted line, as many owners were still reeling from the steep downturn in property values.

They had a short time horizon, and I maintained a much longer one. Their finish line was approaching fast, and mine was stretching way out in the distance. And that essential fact made all the difference in the world.

I refused to be greedy. I never went in as an agent or tried to make a commission on my purchases. I let the Realtors make their money. But that's not to say I didn't make some funding mistakes along the way.

I knew if I walked into my bank and applied for all these mortgages under one name, they'd laugh me right out of the building.

So I approached outside investors and paid them a fee to take out mortgages and hold them in trust for me.

In the short term, my "financial wizardry," as my father called it, worked like a charm. And after I was done assembling, I started building new homes on my newly acquired land, beginning in 1997.

Georgian Bay now looked like a giant Monopoly board. Instead of placing those little plastic red hotels on the game board, I took out construction financing and built five homes, scattering them across what was now a 280-acre parcel.

They were nice homes. I used a fixed blueprint to keep the costs down. Then I called an appraiser out to take a look. I directed his attention to the five new homes I'd just built and handed him the land deeds for each of them.

The paperwork showed that each home came with a deeded right to beach access on the original fifty-acre parcel that was acquired, which boasts seven hundred feet of beach frontage on Georgian Bay. This enabled each house to be classified as a waterfront property.

The appraisals for my homes now rose dramatically in value, which helped me to gather enough money to return to buy my family out of their Georgian Bay investment.

When I told my father of my plan, he'd attempted to dissuade me from going through with it. He didn't want me to take on that level of risk at such a young age.

After all, the weight of a still-depressed market and all the litigation had begun to take a toll on him. He was emotionally spent. But I was my own man who was developing my own discrete business philosophies, so I pushed ahead with my plan anyway.

I felt an overwhelming sense of relief when I finally phoned the lawyers representing my family and informed them I'd be writing them a check. They were free.

They would get their original investment back, which valued the land at $1.2 million. I felt a sense of accomplishment, but it was also mixed with some anger too. The second message I hoped to deliver, albeit on a lower frequency, was *Here's your money. You got exactly what you asked for. Now, go away. Send the lawyers home, and let's get back to our daily lives minus all the vituperation and rancor.*

Things were looking up. While I was busy purchasing all my adjoining parcels in Georgian Bay, my real estate projects in Toronto were growing at a phenomenal rate. Things had taken off so quickly that I'd asked my uncle to partner with me on launching a new construction company to keep up with the surging demand for renovations projects for my properties and for my buyers.

There were still plenty of renters in Toronto who wanted to become homeowners. What had begun for me with a $25,000 basement renovation on a single home owned by Mr. and Mrs. Rankin in Richmond Hills was now blossoming into a multimillion-dollar-a-year cash-flow business.

I had a steady stream of capital coming in via my buyer's program and long-term aspirations for Georgian Bay.

After a moment of relief, however, came real danger. And I learned about **Pillar No. 9: Never put all your eggs—especially your real estate financing—in one basket.**

As much progress as I'd made up to this point, I'd also made one particularly harmful self-inflicted error.

The bankers I was dealing with at the time wound up getting burned by a group of borrowers who either (a) struggled to pay their mortgages or (b) engaged in illicit quick-buck schemes that blew up in their faces.

It didn't matter that I'd paid every one of my mortgage payments on time; the bank's executives panicked. I had borrowed a great deal of money and was deploying properties in a lot of different places, which terrified them.

Bankers are not, by nature, calm and collected thinkers when it comes to real estate. When some of the bank managers were suspended for their bad judgment, panic set in among the top brass. A decision was quickly made to start calling in mortgages all over the place, including all of mine.

That was one phone call I'll never forget. It's not every day that a bank informs you that it is pulling all of your loans. It didn't matter to them that I was in the midst of developing some truly incredible sites in Toronto. The bank wanted its money back. And it wanted it back now.

I remember breaking out in the worst cold sweat of my life that night, followed by a spell of night terrors that haunted me for months. The bank gave me just ten days to come up with the money to cover the loans. Plus, I'd been forced to place four lawyers on retainer to provide me advice.

Looking back, it was almost an impossible situation to navigate.

But I remained loyal to my vision for Georgian Bay and remained committed to ensuring that the people who took those mortgages out for me didn't get burned. What it came down to, for me, was personal credibility.

I could have walked and left those people to deal with the fallout themselves—which would have forced a sale of the parcels. Then, I could have swooped back in later and repurchased them for a song.

That would have been the shrewd business move, but not the honorable decision, because establishing and brokering trust is vital in this business—as is maintaining one's hard-built reputation. I had a track record of paying my debts, so I refused to take the easy way out.

At night I didn't get much sleep. But when the sun was shining, I hit the bricks. I visited every bank that would let me in for a consultation and started refinancing as many of my projects as humanly possible.

Although I had to liquidate some of my rental properties, which would be worth a fortune today, I solved most of my mortgage issues and never looked back.

Given that Georgian Bay was the riskiest property in my portfolio, no banks would cover the costs associated with that property. I needed extra help to hold on to that land, which came in the form of an angel investor.

To this day I view private financing as a last resort. But if I'm to be honest, I don't know if anyone else, besides this individual, would've backed me and helped me save my Georgian Bay properties. But he did, and I learned a great deal from him in the process.

That being said, I took on a great deal of risk, too, by accepting his offer, which was a bit of an uneven deal. No lawyer giving independent legal advice would have ever encouraged me to sign it, but I did anyway.

My angel investor's only reason for advancing these funds was my unassailable credibility. And in the end, given the way he'd structured the contract, it wound up being, in my opinion, an extraordinarily lucrative deal for him, as the equity position also had an interest-carrying component for every penny that he advanced. I had also provided additional security outside of the Georgian Bay parcel to secure any monies advanced.

It worked out because I spent the next three years working tirelessly to amplify the value of those parcels. I rented out homes on that land as the prices stabilized.

By 2002 I'd devised an escape plan. The caring costs for those properties were rising, and I wanted to cut costs after a great run.

I knew that the Planning Act of Ontario allowed property owners to sell their parcel of land to an interested owner but write an option into the contract that allowed them to buy back portions of the original parcel of land in no more than twenty-one years minus one day.

This agreement would be registered on title and run with the land for twenty-one years less a day. Any new buyer would inherit the terms of this agreement. I retained the ownership of the original fifty-acre beachfront parcel, but I could sell the adjoining plots of land that I'd amassed around it. So I found several buyers willing to acquire the different parcels. The terms of this option agreement registered on title effectively allowed me to sever most of the acreage of land except the newly constructed house and one acre. The balance of the acreage would be deeded back to me for $1 if I was successful with the land severance, which for clarification would amount to 230 acres less five acres and the five houses equating to 225 acres deeded back to me for $1. I unloaded it and waited patiently.

I knew it was going to take time for Georgian Bay to mature into a vacation destination. So I felt it was best to sit back and see if my instincts would prove correct.

And sure enough, as I waited, interest in reimagining Georgian Bay into a vacation destination began to gain more traction. The project that went into receivership in Victoria Harbor in the late 1980s became a successful waterfront development a decade later. Projects in Port McNicol started to take traction, and then in 2015 a massive development called Friday Harbor took root in Innisfil, Ontario, not far from Georgian Bay.

And as everyone knows, the best location to open one car dealership is next to another. And thus the best place to build one high-end vacation resort is within driving distance of another. The COVID-19 era also drove cottage properties up as the stress of lockdowns created a demand and appreciation for our precious waterways like never before.

In regard to my options agreements, I kept delaying the land severance application—for eighteen years—until it became clear that my ability to exercise the option was running out.

I knew that this application process was going to be risky and quite frankly an uphill battle. We not only had to make a strong case, but it would also cost me a lot of money to do so.

I also knew I'd likely be called before the Ontario Land Tribunal (OLT), which meant the consultants I'd hired could charge by the hour. Add up the costs required for my lawyers as well as various planners and consultants to participate in this process, and I was looking at a rough cost of $3,000 per hour, which is what I wound up paying.

When you are unable to secure council approval on a planning application, you have to turn to the OLT, which invariably wants to see a positive planning report.

In this case I did not have a positive planning report. So it's no surprise that Simcoe County decided to fight me every step of the way. The county argued that these parcels were located in rural areas—thus the planning parameters did not allow for development outside the settlement areas.

Nevertheless, we pressed on. Although our initial arguments didn't prove successful, we eventually settled on one strategy that did work out.

I had a landlocked piece of real estate that would physically connect to a series of parcels that I was trying to sever. The additional lot creation in this case was zero. It did not connect all of them. I did have to withdraw some of my applications, however, before I managed to negotiate the settlement. Given the lot creation was zero, there were no new developments, and therefore we utilized a section of the official plan, which allows for lot realignments.

This settlement agreement basically deeded me 180 acres of land that are very rich in minerals and aggregates for a nominal fee of one dollar. On December 8, 2022, the chair for the OLT approved my severances. On May 29, 2023, after satisfying all the conditions of the approval and with only seventeen days to go on my options before they expired, 180 acres of land was deeded back to me for a nominal fee of $1. These lands accompanied by the original parcel of 50 acres of beach front property equates to over 230 acres of land. The returns on these parcels could result in millions of dollars in profits, either by moving forward with my original beach club golf course resort concept or via profits accrued from mining.

Which finally leads us to **Pillar No. 10: Everyone knows the golden rule of real estate is location, location, location. But I'd argue that its corollary—purpose, purpose, purpose—is just as important.**

Like any other real estate investment, nothing is written in stone. But it's thrilling to think that both my father's and my vision for Georgian Bay may become a reality in the years to come.

CHAPTER 2

THINK LIKE A BUYER

What better way to launch into a discussion about being a buyer's agent than by addressing, head on, all the well-worn clichés about buyers?

When I was coming up in the industry in the 1990s, sellers' agents didn't have anything nice to say about buyers at all.

All buyers are liars, kid. That's what all the old-timers told me. *They're wishy-washy and fickle—can't make a decision to save their lives.*

They'll ask you to drive them all around town like a glorified cabbie, and then once the gas money is spent, they'll say, "Sorry, nothing's striking my fancy."

And if they did actually like a property? I was told to prepare myself to be carpet-bombed with thousands of questions.

"Buyers," I was warned, "exist for no other reason than to drive real estate agents batty."

I'm here to argue the opposite position. Namely that buyers aren't only a young real estate agent's greatest asset, but they are also the secret to a swift ascent up the ladder.

After all, the opportunity for real estate agents to represent buyers is a relatively new phenomenon, which only became available in 1995.

In years past if you were a real estate agent, you were paid to represent sellers. Whoever owned a piece of land or home was the one who paid your commission. Buyers were, therefore, viewed as a necessary evil.

Then, of course, the industry's regulations evolved, allowing us to be buyers' agents. And this brave new real estate world left long-established Realtors feeling spiteful and nervous about their prospects.

So what did they do? Naturally, they lashed out at what they didn't yet understand.

That chief critique of buyers, both then and now, is that they can be awfully fickle people. For a host of reasons—some logical, some nonsensical—they can drop you as their agent and hire someone else, leaving you nothing to show for months' worth of hustle and paper cuts.

I was told that if I represented buyers, I'd eventually get screwed over—so many times, in so many different ways—that I'd go jetting back to the seller's side like a bat straight out of Hades.

> **The single most-effective way to begin one's career in real estate is by representing buyers before migrating into the seller's world.**

Of course, those were gross exaggerations, which obscured a far more important pearl of wisdom that's worth noting: truth is, the single most-effective way to begin one's career in real estate is by representing buyers before migrating into the seller's world.

Today, my brokerage happily represents both buyers and sellers, but I encourage my new agents to start on the buyer's side.

Yes, it's true: some buyers are liars. Some won't respect your time or efforts. And some can be evasive or indecisive. But representing buyers allows you not only to get your foot in the door but also to kick that door straight off its hinges.

Why? Because helping others find and purchase great properties will help you learn to buy great real estate for *yourself*. Good buyer agents tend to evolve into good real estate investors.

Let me put it this way: *if you cultivate a reputation for being able to generate immediate and long-term wealth for your clients, you can look at yourself in the mirror every morning and know, with relative certainty, that you have the ability to do the same for yourself.*

And with that self-assurance—that little voice in your head that says, "I made it happen for them, so I can make it happen for me"—comes glorious opportunities.

After all, buyers are tasked not only with scouting property but also with helping clients figure how they are going to pay for them. In contrast a seller's job is monolithic: the goal is to sell the home in question for the highest price possible.

As a buyer's agent, you can hone critical skill more quickly than as a seller's agent, especially how to assess the *real* value of a given property.

Your client will expect you to be a font of knowledge regarding the quality of the local school system, crime rates, zoning issues, and transportation options. The list of queries is virtually endless. And in fielding those questions, you wind up educating yourself while educating others.

Is it easier to represent buyers than sellers? No, it's probably, in aggregate, harder work. But you're likely to learn a great deal more in a shorter period of time about the things that really matter, like drafting offers, working with sticky leases, talking to selling agents, and so on.

You'll quickly learn, for instance, that purchasing the worst house on a stellar block is always better than a best house in a bad neighborhood. Working with buyers will also reinforce the fact that the best lead generators are personal referrals. That was true fifty years ago. It's true today. And it will continue to be true 150 years from now.

In short being a buyer's agent will help you become a better seller and a better real estate developer. And while the inverse can also be true, it's not generally true to the same degree.

If you're a buyer, you have to think like a generalist. If you're a seller's agent, you're better served being a specialist.

After all, some of the most remarkable seller agents in our business have succeeded by narrowing their scope. It's harder to break into some high-net-worth areas because other real estate agents have essentially cornered that market. They've made fortunes by remaining laser focused on understanding the psychology of a particular set of buyers who live in a particular set of communities.

There's certainly nothing wrong with that business model. I tip my cap to those who've done so. After all, if you own a home in a glittering neighborhood and want to sell, why wouldn't you want to hire someone who has experience maxing out the value of the properties in that area?

The problem, of course, is that many sellers lock themselves inside gilded cages of their own choosing. And as someone new to the field, you don't want to limit your knowledge to any one area of a city. You want to learn about as many different neighborhoods, geographies, and properties as possible.

I encourage all our young real estate agents to explore beyond their own backyards and survey the whole map. My directive: "Go out into the world and see what else is out there."

There's a reason, for instance, why I've acquired land and properties beyond my home turf of Richmond Hills, Ontario. I've been able to diversify my portfolio because, as a young agent, I drove buyers from one edge of greater Toronto to the other.

Richmond Hill. Newmarket. Toronto. Durham. York. Simcoe County. Georgian Bay. Wherever my clients took me in Ontario. I didn't focus on just one discrete area. I expanded my sights, intent on finding properties that could generate immediate wealth for my clients wherever I could find them.

And, over time, I used that bank of knowledge to buy the right properties and build wealth for myself. The phrase "no sell, only buy" became entrenched in my DNA, and it is the common characteristic of the most successful wealth-creating investor moguls.

That's not to say that I don't have plenty of horror stories to share. For example, I remember, early in my career, working with a South African couple that was looking for a new home in Richmond Hill.

I'd devoted so much of my time to finding them their dream home that I made a serious error, the kind of slap-your-forehead mistake that countless young real estate agents continue to make to this day.

I'd begun my work without securing a signed buyer's agreement, which wound up costing me dearly.

Even when I did find this couple a perfect home, they were concerned, as so many buyers are, about whether they could afford the property. So I sat down, crunched the numbers, and drew up a plan for how they could buy the house with very little money down.

That turned out to be a major mistake, as they "borrowed" my ideas, went behind my back, and hired a different buyer's agent, who bought a different property using the exact same financing plan I had drawn up.

I felt gutted by the experience. Losing a deal that you've poured your heart and soul into is beyond demoralizing. But if there was a silver lining to the whole adventure, it was that my financing plan had obviously been effective enough that someone else felt the need to steal it.

My advice to you? Ascend the ladder, one rung after the other. Don't try to cut any corners. You can certainly begin your career by representing sellers, but why try and take a shortcut, when helping buyers will get you to your end goal far more quickly?

After all, you have to learn how to skate before you can play hockey, right? If you're a young hockey player and want to take your skills to the next level, what's your best strategy? Do you want to keep skating in your hometown league where you're going to play the same opponents and same teams over and over again, season after season? Or would you rather challenge yourself by playing the teams who have more talent and more play-making abilities?

Why stay cloistered, locked inside a bubble, when you can acquire far more knowledge and experiences by venturing outside of it?

Trust me: all that blood, sweat, tears, and frustration will pay off in ways you'd never expect them to.

It certainly did for me. And there's nothing stopping you from doing the same, especially if you tackle your career ascent in the following order:

Step One: Find the Right Broker

This is a slightly more polished way of saying, "Shop around until you find yourself a proper mentor."

If your broker's face is plastered on the side of buses, on billboards, and across public benches, I'd be very cautious about signing up to be on their team.

Thirst for public notoriety isn't just a red flag; it's an air raid siren bellowing *my ego outweighs my financial acumen.*

As a young agent, you never want your boss to be obsessed with selling, because if they're spending all their time chasing down deals, who's going to help you become a better agent?

You don't want to partner with a broker who is selfish and consumed with their own public image. If you find yourself, as an agent, in a competitive-offer situation with your own broker and wind up losing out to them, that's a gut-wrenching feeling.

Strong leaders don't try to take credit for other people's success; they work inconspicuously, behind the scenes, to enable others to achieve their potential. If your new boss is focused on the cosmetic side of this business and prattles on about their market share or how "they're number one," you're setting yourself up for disappointment.

Big balloons aren't worth the helium it takes to fill them. Trust me when I say they float high and pop quickly.

Instead, look for someone who can look you square in the eyes and tell you, "Our goal is to do everything possible to ensure you become a shooting star in this marketplace." *That's* the kind of person you want to go into battle with—someone who's going to teach you and support you when you need it most.

I recommend asking all potential employers to explain, in great detail, four key aspects of their brokerage operations: their training platform, marketing efforts, lead-generation strategies, and client service.

Don't be fooled by numbers, especially talk of "market share." Some brands will try to claim that they have the greatest market share. That's nonsense. We all have the same market share as real estate agents because, when we go on the MLS, we all have the exact same access to listings as any other real estate agent.

What people want to know is this: What is your track record in terms of service? What can you do for *them*?

Make sure a brokerage's interests are tied to your success. We don't, for instance, see a penny, at The Real Estate Centre (TREC), unless our Realtors make a sale. We ensure that they receive the proper training at no cost. We don't charge them a penny to train them, help them market themselves, or generate leads. We see it as our responsibility to try and transform every individual who joins our business into a first-class Realtor.

When you're new to this industry, the right broker can accelerate your growth or stunt it. Be mindful of the paid recruiters. It's going to seem, at first blush, like they have all the right answers. They're going to say all the right things. They're going to sound slick. And they are going to make you feel really good about their business model.

But remember: you want to make a smart decision, not an emotional decision. You have to read between the lines. In many cases they are really in it for the monthly desk fees that go onto your credit card every month.

Our motto at TREC is "We Are Your Agent-First Brokerage." You won't see our pictures plastered everywhere. We want our Realtors to be leaders in the marketplace. What we've built is a safe place to share ideas, whether they are personal or professional. We work collaboratively. And our culture allows you to be a part of something bigger. We're a family. We recognize and encourage you to develop your own branding and form your own identity. It's not about us. It's about you.

Step Two: Transform Renters into Buyers

New real estate agents often dream of working for wealthy clients and dealing with exclusive properties. They think if they can hook one big score, the money will come rolling in forevermore.

For most this rags-to-riches plan proves to be nothing more than a pipe dream.

My advice: start out small, working the basement units and ranches, and the top-floor penthouses will come in due time.

In the beginning your greatest gains will come by working in less-desirable neighborhoods and representing average renters who aspire to become homeowners. Try turning the people and places that snooty real estate agents write off as the "nothings" into "somethings" of real value.

When my grandfather immigrated to Canada and settled where every other Italian in Toronto set down roots, near St. Clair College, he left abject poverty back in the Old Country. In Italy his family lived in a shack perched high up in the mountains. He'd worked as a farmer for pauper's wages. But he dreamed, as every immigrant does, of owning a little piece of land that he could call his own.

So whenever I drove through working-class neighborhoods, I saw people who reminded me of my grandfather. They shared the same dream, only they held them during different moments in time.

> **Try turning the people and places that snooty real estate agents write off as the "nothings" into "somethings" of real value.**

I owe a great deal of my success to hardworking families who trusted me to help them find and finance the purchase of their first homes. And you should do it too, and if you come through for them, you'll make yourself a friend for life.

In the 1990s I represented many renters who lived in impoverished areas in the greater Toronto area. Why did so many flock to me?

Because I helped them generate wealth immediately.

How did I manage to achieve that? By teaching them how they could renovate a portion of their new home and rent it out, thereby generating instantaneous income.

It's exciting for a renter to become a homeowner, but it's twice as exhilarating to transition from being a renter to being a landlord in one fell swoop.

That's what I did for my very first clients, Mr. and Mrs. Rankin, who bought a place in Richmond Hill and quickly converted their new basement into a rental unit.

At the time there was a little-known initiative called the purchase plus improvement program, which was being run by insurers who specialized in high-ratio mortgages. The purchase plus program allowed the Rankins to obtain a mortgage based on the initial value of their new home, prior to any renovations. That initial mortgage, however, could be revised upward to include additional renovation costs and bundled into an all-in-one mortgage.

Under the program, renovations could begin as soon as the sale was completed—albeit with one small catch: the renovation portion of this bundle would be held back by the bank upon closing and released when, and only when, one of its inspectors verified that the work was properly completed.

This addendum didn't concern me a bit, because my uncle and I supervised those renovations for the Rankins.

And sure enough, when the work was completed, we received high marks from the inspector. The check was cut by the bank. We were paid. And Mrs. Rankin celebrated.

Over the years I've devised all sorts of interesting financing deals, all legal and above board, to reduce the total costs for my clients. For instance, we often hired homeowners or members of their family to work as subcontractors so they could earn back part of their own down payment.

Skilled hands could help us with serious work, like demolition, while others might handle simple carpentry jobs or hang drywall. And those without any handyman skill whatsoever could always help paint or toil away on odd jobs.

Whatever it would cost me to complete that particular task was then paid directly to the homeowner who performed the work.

As a young real estate agent, you have to hustle. You have to think outside the box. You have to define a problem and solve it. One of my favorite mantras, to this very day, is just three words in length: *make it happen.*

Put your head down and find a way to make things happen, even when the odds are stacked against you. Because if you do "make things happen," if you find a way to make something out of nothing, who do you think your clients are going to call to sell their house years later?

They're going to call you. Doesn't matter who comes knocking at their front door, offering to sell their house. Doesn't matter if someone else sends them a fancy marketing brochure or inundates their inbox with emails. They're going to remember *you.* They're going to remember all the hard work that you put into being the best buyer's agent possible and ask you to be their seller's agent too.

Step Three: Treat Your Clients Like Extended Members of the Family

When I was a young boy, my grandfather gave me an extraordinary gift. It wasn't a family heirloom or a memento. He shared an old Italian saying with me: *Quando le tue mani sono spaventate come i tuoi occhi, niente verrà fatto.* Roughly translated it means if your hands are as afraid as your eyes, nothing will ever get done.

As a buyer's agent, you need to prioritize the needs and interests of your client above all else. In other words you have a responsibility to consider their best interest. This includes 100 percent confidentiality. You must disclose any and all pertinent information that might affect their decision-making process. You are responsible for making good-faith disclosures. And you owe your clients competency, loyalty, and good faith.

Those are the simple oaths you must swear to uphold as a buyer's agent. But my grandfather's shrewd little maxim provided me greater clarity as to what I should be doing beyond those commandments.

We all know that buying a new home can be a stressful experience. And thus buyers are always circumspect about taking a leap. They are afraid to commit. They are afraid to take on more debt. They are afraid of moving into a new neighborhood. Suffice to say they're often afraid of change.

But here's the thing: they want to talk to *you*, as their buyer's agent, about those fears. I don't mean a five- or ten-minute conversation; I mean hour-long conversations. It's your job to listen and gain their trust, to build a solid rapport with them. If a client doesn't feel the urge, whether spoken or unspoken, to call you a friend at the end of the process, you obviously didn't do enough to earn their trust.

My advice: make a concerted effort to lessen the fear in people's minds by dazzling their eyes. Take the time to drive them all over the place to see different homes and properties. Walk them down from the ledge when they show doubt. Hold their hands, metaphorically and literally speaking, as you explain different financing options to them.

Trust me when I say that soft skills matter. They really matter. I offer you, as proof, the story of an early client of mine, a single mother whom we'll call Ruth.

Ruth was struggling to make ends meet and purchase a new house, so I suggested she create a rentable basement apartment with access to her garage.

Normally, homeowners pay for their own permits, but Ruth didn't have enough money to cover them. So I stepped in and put up the money for her. I also personally guided her through the entire approval process.

Sometimes, real estate agents can't see the forest for the trees. While there are some buyers who take great glee at being extortionists—crying poverty to try and grab some free money—Ruth clearly wasn't one of those people.

So trust your radar. In some cases taking a hardline approach might be necessary, but when you're working with a quality client, putting up a little of your own money will win you a client for life and sterling referrals for the rest of your career.

On this particular project, I knew we'd have some tricky zoning issues to deal with. But what we didn't realize was that we'd be saddled with a building inspector who'd show up to our work site every week looking for something to critique.

Suffice to say Ruth and I persevered. I was punctilious in ensuring the work was completed both quickly and correctly. By the end of the project, the inspector had no choice but to approve it.

Ruth was overjoyed. And to be honest, it felt really good to know that we'd done a little something to give her daughter a head start in life.

It's very simple, isn't it? Take care of your clients, and they'll take care of you.

That's how you build a reputation in this industry: you go the extra mile for your clients. You build a name for yourself by convincing trustworthy people to trust you.

And sure enough, years later, I received a phone call from a man I'd never met before. He'd called me out of the blue. He said, "I don't know you, but I have a friend named Ruth. When I told her about my problem, she told me to immediately hang up the phone and dial you."

Then the man said something I still cherish to this day: "Ruth tells me she would never be where she is today if it weren't for you."

Step Four: Don't Be Afraid to Paint Outside the Lines

Once you've established a stable of quality clients, you can use that safety net to begin taking some chances. I realize that my willingness to take on risks is higher than most people. But I maintain that taking risks, whether small ones or major ones, is necessary for true growth.

During my early years, I took a lot of risks. I pioneered the first no-money-down programs in Canada, and I was the first to take advantage of adding the costs of renovations to people's mortgages when they bought a home. In fact, by 2003 many mortgage insurers and banks debuted their own no-money-down financing options that were exact clones of my own.

But one of my more unconventional marketing strategies came as a result of seeing so many sellers' agents' signs staked in people's front yards. There wasn't a single buyer's agent sign, however, anywhere to be seen.

Given my background in sales, I understood the importance of signage. In my opinion it was free advertising.

Why, I wondered, couldn't buyers' agents do the same?

I decided to ask every buyer I represented to place a sign with my name on it in their new front lawns and keep it there for sixty days. Turns out they were more than happy to do so.

At the time, buyers' agents simply didn't do such things—and most still don't even to this day. But I forged ahead anyway, creating something of an uproar.

Shortly after planting my first sign, I learned from a friend that a sales-side broker in Newmarket had sent out a group email to her entire office that said, "If anyone is thinking about doing a deal with Dean Artenosi, you have to call me first to approve it."

It just so happened that this broker was working for the same national brand but a different independent brokerage that I was working for at the time. I knew I couldn't let this go unchecked, so I drove straight to her office, walked in the front door, and told her secretary I was here to see her boss.

The front-desk manager nervously picked up the phone and relayed the message. A door swung opened, followed by the broker, who was already fumbling her words by the time I crossed the threshold into her office.

I was angry as hell on the inside but remained calm on the outside. I reiterated what I'd heard and asked her point blank if it was true.

She nodded her head yes.

I asked her two follow-up questions: number one, I wanted to know why she objected to me putting up my own signs. And number two, why did she email every member of her team and tell them they had to clear deals with her first?

That was all it took. She melted. As the sweat began to pool on her forehead, she said she should have been more precise with her words. That she'd made a mistake in opposing my right to post my own signage.

And then she said, "Actually, I don't have any problem whatsoever with you putting up signs anymore."

I tell this story not to try and exact any revenge so much as to drive the point home that ego and irrational jealousies have always been prevalent in our business and always will be. You can't bend to them. You have every right to work within

Work within the rules of the system and try new things. Get creative with your financing. Adopt unorthodox marketing campaigns. Prioritize first-time home buyers.

the rules of the system and try new things. Get creative with your financing. Adopt unorthodox marketing campaigns. Prioritize first-time home buyers.

Don't be afraid to draw outside the lines.

Building a Rolodex of trusted clients gives you the freedom to zig when everyone else is zagging. When you look back, years hence, it's the risks that you took early in your career that are likely to be the real difference makers.

It's less important to trumpet your personal successes than create real wealth for your clients. For instance, I catapulted my sales practice into the top 1 percent of all Canadian real estate agents when I was a very young Realtor. But this was less important to me than the fact that I started with nothing and built something of real substance out of it—both for my clients and my own business.

The true gratification, in this business, comes from creating long-term wealth. Which brings us to the final step.

Step Five: Build On Your Prior Successes

Success is like piling up building blocks, one atop the other. With new skills come greater confidence. And with confidence comes a greater appetite to take risks. And with those new risks tend to come outsized rewards. And with huge gains you develop a certain degree of fear-lessness. Over time the things that scare others away from pursuing monster deals aren't going to frighten you away in the least.

Which is why it's incumbent upon you to do the little things that most people overlook. Some are so self-evident that I'm shocked so many people neglect them.

No. 1: Ask for Referrals

If you work for someone and they're satisfied with your work, ask them for a list of friends and family members who might need your help as well.

Not only should you build a client database, but you should also keep in touch with them by sticking to a robust client-engagement plan.

No. 2: Spend Money on the Right Kind of Advertising

There's no need to be ostentatious about your marketing efforts and put your face in every ad, but there's no doubt that strategic Facebook, Google, and other social media advertising campaigns work. So allocate a portion of your resources to advertising, and be diligent about following through on your ad spends, no matter the circumstances.

No. 3: Keep Training

Just as I recommend new agents find a broker who offers a tiered training program, I think everyone in real estate, no matter their experience, should continually educate themselves by attending training opportunities.

Some Realtors say they don't have enough time for more training or to drop into sales seminars, company meetings, and the like. That's the wrong approach. If it's success you're chasing, it invariably requires continual self-development.

No. 4: Ignore the Distractions

Why do so many young real estate agents throw in the towel, just as they are beginning to build momentum? Because they fear the unknown. They fear new technology. Or they fear that what they achieved on a small scale can't be replicated on a larger one.

Take it from me: there's always going to be some irrational fear that sends shivers up the spine of the entire industry. When I was coming up, people said that the internet would render our business obsolete. That it would usher in a new wave of "for sale by owner" deals that would drown us all.

That proved to be a red herring, a baseless fear, just like so many other "the sky is falling" panics that have come and gone. Focus on the process. Focus on what you've already achieved, and keep working. The more you stay in the fight, the more tenacious and confident you'll become in the later rounds.

No. 5: Remember Your Purpose

Never lose sight of your ultimate objective, which is to build a solid sales practice and real estate portfolio. Your job, whether you're representing a buyer or seller, is to solve people's problems and assuage their fears by offering them an ultimate service. In short it's your job to help them build wealth—profits in the short and long term.

The truth of the matter is that success in this business is accretive. Let's say you successfully represent buyers, and you earn their trust. Think about what that's going to mean for you when you do migrate into representing sellers and listings.

When you attempt to sell someone's house, you're going to possess a ready store of wisdom about a lot of buyers. I can recount countless stories, throughout my career, when I represented a seller and didn't even have to put their house on the MLS because I knew I could easily play matchmaker between that house and a former client. I knew my old clients well enough to know that their tastes were going to perfectly align with what that new property had to offer them.

And thus being a good buyer's agent will make you a good seller's agent. And if you manage to gain experience doing both, there's no reason you can't use it to become a real estate investor yourself, which is the focus of our next chapter.

CHAPTER 3

HOW TO BUILD A SUCCESSFUL REAL ESTATE PORTFOLIO

As I've already stressed, representing the interests of buyers is an indispensable first step in becoming a successful real estate investor. Spend enough time acquiring income-producing properties for other people, and you'll be able to do the same for yourself.

After working with buyers, you should be able to do all the following:

- Properly establish a fair market value for a given property

- Analyze the pros and cons of investing in different areas and neighborhoods

- Recognize the long-term value of changing the use of different sites and parcels

- Leverage creative financing strategies to acquire properties and renovate them in the short term

If you can do all the above, there's a strong likelihood you'll be able to identify overlooked buying opportunities that sellers' agents won't have the time or inclination to pursue.

So I implore you: don't be scared of taking on difficult clients or accepting challenging real estate searches. I've found that the most stressful jobs are far more beneficial to your long-term development than the simple ones. And the more experienced you become in devising detailed renovation projects for your clients, the more likely you'll be to do the same for yourself.

So remember this golden rule: when you're building a real estate portfolio—whether modest or ambitious—purchase properties that enable you to make money the moment you take possession of them. Your goal isn't just to generate long-term wealth but to make money *immediately* after purchasing the property.

When you're building a real estate portfolio— whether modest or ambitious—purchase properties that enable you to make money the moment you take possession of them.

Which is why I consider real estate investing to be more of an art than a craft. You have to develop a feel for it—an ability to see past what a property is today and foresee what it could become over time.

There is no magic recipe for success. No immaculately illustrated how-to manual. There are simply too many variables—different properties, different parcels, different neighborhoods, different circumstances—to reduce real estate investing down to a simple plug-and-play formula.

The question worth asking yourself, before you make a single move, is this: Do I have the resilience needed to persevere when others will throw in the towel and bail? Can I remain calm when I find myself swept up in a whirlwind of adversity and stress? Can I make the difficult decisions when every fiber of my being is imploring me to make the easy ones?

What you need, above all else, is good old-fashioned resilience because you will inevitably experience setbacks. You will hit rough patches. Things won't always go as planned. Inevitably, you will suffer through bouts of angst and uncertainty.

The key is to fight through them. My hope is that by sharing some of the challenges I faced while developing my early real estate portfolio, you'll be able to steel yourself against self-doubt and hold the line.

So what's the first step when you're ready to take the leap? Start by asking yourself this question: Am I in the proper frame of mind to begin this journey?

Whenever I hire new Realtors to join TREC, I look for two qualities above all else: curiosity and creativity. Paperwork is paperwork. Sales are sales. Presentation skills can be taught, as can the analysis required to properly evaluate a property's worth.

That being said, if I meet someone who shows a willingness to understand what motivates people—or what makes some neighborhoods flourish and others stagnate—I immediately perk up. The same goes for anyone with an aptitude for thinking outside the box when it comes to creative financing.

In short I'll always take an inexperienced problem solver over a rigid thinker. We all have our own unique ways of getting our creative juices flowing, so start with your own personal catalysts. Prime the pump. Whatever you need to do—activities, hobbies, podcasts, reading materials—to activate your curiosity, start doing it. And commit yourself to making those rituals a part of your daily routine.

Because, in my experience, innately curious people are less intimidated by the prospect of taking risks and exploring new neighborhoods.

When you're starting out, focus your attention on transitioning neighborhoods that have the potential to blossom into desirable ones.

When I was a young buyer's agent, I worked in a diverse cross section of neighborhoods across the Toronto area. If someone tacked a huge map of the area onto a wall, closed their eyes, and threw a dart, it would be impossible to hit an area I hadn't studied.

I've owned, invested in, and sold properties throughout greater Toronto. East and west. Up to York and into suburbs like Newmarket, Aurora, and Richmond Hill. I went further north into towns within Simcoe County, from Barrie and Innisfil to Gravenhurst. And I continued to look for properties far beyond Toronto, surveying Tay Township and towns across the Northeast.

Aurora, Ontario, for instance, was flush with post–World War II bungalows and two-story semidetached homes. And a particular neighborhood in Newmarket, the Dogpatch I mentioned previously, was overflowing with low-income renters who longed to be homeowners.

I became knowledgeable about as many places as possible, because one of the best ways to increase your sales is to work in multiple markets at the same time. So move around, and remember: make sure to look in all the unusual places.

Finding a good piece of real estate can be a lot like unpacking a set of Russian nesting dolls. The best prizes are often found hidden inside subregions of overlooked neighborhoods or on the outskirts or established ones, where no one else has bothered to look.

Sometimes, it's less about the neighborhood itself than little pockets of promise nestled within it, so explore subdivisions and individual blocks that are beginning to enjoy increased foot traffic.

When you possess limited investment capital, you should also look for neighborhoods that seem to be teetering between stasis and growth. On the one hand, you might understand why some people might have reservations about moving there. On the other hand, you might be able to imagine why others might jump at the chance to set down roots there.

Anyone with a great deal of capital can invest in wealthy enclaves or tourist hubs, but there's a real art in discovering neighborhoods that are poised for a renaissance.

If you're struggling to find a worthy neighborhood, consider visiting your nearest university town. You can learn a great deal about the psyche of renters by spending time in a place that's teeming with undergraduates.

Case in point: in the late 1990s, my brother was accepted into McGill University in Montreal. Knowing he needed a place to live, I cosigned on a $120,000 three-bedroom unit for him.

We took advantage of a high-ratio government mortgage financing option from the Canada Mortgage Housing Corporation, which enabled him to buy the property while only putting 5 percent down.

Then we devised how he could *immediately* generate income. Although renting out two of his three bedrooms would cover his mortgage costs, renting out his third bedroom would provide him extra spending money.

So we converted the unit's living room into a fourth bedroom. In the end it cost a few thousand dollars but was worth every penny, as this passive income stream allowed him to enjoy all that Montreal had to offer while he was still a university student.

After a few years, my brother received a call from an investor who was on the prowl for a four-bedroom space in a neighborhood overcrowded with two- and three-bedroom units.

My brother's flat fit the bill. Negotiations ensued. And in short order, my brother sold him the building for $275,000, essentially doubling his investment in four years, not to mention the fact that his rental income paid for all of his accommodations during the four years he went to university.

Rather than graduating with hundreds of thousands in student debt, he left McGill with a surplus of cash, which he quickly used to buy a subsequent property, effectively beginning the cycle all over again.

I recognize that this is a story about a modest investment that yielded modest returns, but I'd argue those are *precisely* the kind of projects you want to pursue when you're just starting out. The key is to create an investment checklist and carefully follow it.

My own personal to-do list looks something like this:

- Do I thoroughly understand the pros and cons—the perils and the promise—of the neighborhood I'm investing in?

- Have I been creative in terms of financing the purchase and/or renovations?

- Have I carefully examined how I might change the use of an existing property to bolster its long-term value?

- Have I devised a detailed plan that enables me to create a steady stream of income as soon as I take possession of the property?

- Am I putting myself in a position to be able to hold out long enough to sell the property for a sizable profit in the future?

When you take all the above considerations into account, it's no surprise that I advise new real estate investors to start out by buying and developing properties that are located close to where they already live.

In the United States, you can write off your mortgage payments on your principal residence. You can't do that here in Canada. That being said, you don't get taxed on your principal residence when you sell it in Canada. So why not start out by viewing your own home as a foundational element of your budding real estate portfolio?

Far too many speakers on the real estate circuits encourage investors to purchase properties they really can't afford. My advice? Strongly consider transforming your home into an investment property by devising creative ways to change its use.

One of the first buildings I purchased was a $160,000 property in Toronto—16 Sumach Street. I split the cost with a friend to defray the costs, but the key to our success was a joint commitment to renovating the property.

Given the size and scope of my current work, it was a small project, but I firmly believe that it was my ability to string together a series of small wins early in my career that generated much bigger payoffs down the line.

My friend and I made alterations to our home. We converted our garage into an extra living space, added bathrooms and kitchens, and acted as subcontractors renovating our new purchase. This enabled us to leverage the financing, make money with our purchase by covering all our costs, as well as get our initial investment back. We lived there and rented out portions of the home to friends to carry it. A few years later, we sold that property, earning $150,000 in profit.

No matter where you choose to invest, look for creative financing opportunities. I've already mentioned Canada's purchase plus improvement program, a high-ratio product offered by insurers that allows buyers to bundle the cost of renovations into their mortgage.

But let me also point out an important and still-viable opportunity that continues to benefit buyers in the Ontario area. Any single-family homeowner who can prove that their basement unit included a bedroom, kitchen, and bathroom *prior to 1996* can legally reclassify it as a duplex. All one needs to do is follow proper guidelines and obtain approvals from a fire inspector that the unit is safe for habitation.

This opportunity effectively transforms these units into what we refer to as "legal nonconforming duplexes," meaning they don't have to comply with newer zoning ordinances. This opportunity was very prominent in the late 1990s and early 2000s. Today, another new piece of legislation is coming down the pike from the Ontario government that will allow homeowners to rent out parts of their home or create two or three auxiliary units in their single-family homes. This should create interesting opportunities for new homeowners.

The best strategy for new investors is to buy and sell existing properties rather than new construction. Remember: the value of existing properties is equal to whatever someone else is willing to pay for it.

The sale price of an existing building can fluctuate based on your negotiation skills and good old-fashioned timing. And if you've logged time working with buyers, you can leverage your experience buying homes during depressed markets—and then selling them during boom times—for a massive profit.

In order to maximize your profit, however, you have to find ways to improve its overall value.

My blood runs cold whenever I hear so-called experts prattle on about building teams and downlines. Those are red herrings. You end goal as a real estate investor should be to generate additional wealth throughout the life span of that property.

Although we will devote a whole chapter to new urbanism, I would be remiss not to introduce the topic here, as I wholeheartedly believe in the revitalization of existing communities, as opposed to the construction of new units that erode our precious green fields.

New urbanism is not, if I'm to be frank, a particularly "new" concept. It's a movement that's been with us for decades. It focuses on returning to a way of life that was respected in Europe for centuries. New urbanism supports the development and use of public transportation. But it also advocates for the creation of new synergies, dynamic architecture, and walkable streets, all while preserving the natural beauty of the land surrounding densely packed urban areas.

New urbanism is no fad. It's a laudable and attainable goal, much like sustainable energy, which is deeply embedded in the plans and aspirations of civic leaders, architects, and real estate professionals across the globe. Which is yet another reason why I encourage real estate investors to learn how to change the use of existing properties rather than focus on new construction.

Your ability to accurately assess the value of an existing property—coupled with the creativity and vision needed to revitalize it—will not only be an important skill to develop in today's market, but it will also remain invaluable throughout your career.

For example, I make it a priority to teach novice real estate investors about the extraordinary profits that can be made by assembling individual parcels—I personally love corner lots—and converting them into larger units through a change of use.

As you continue to build your portfolio, learn how to assemble and divide parcels of land. You might consider taking a parcel that once housed four homes and building a six-story building or townhouse development on it. Or if you're just starting out, don't be afraid to think smaller: buy a property that's a hundred feet wide and see if there's value in dividing it into two fifty-foot lots.

Building a strong real estate portfolio—especially one built around the concept of adaptive reuse—is the single most efficient way to generate wealth. But just as it takes money to make money, you will need to make capital investments to generate healthy long-term returns.

I bristle, for instance, whenever a rookie real estate agent says something like, "If you want to make any money on *that* place, you're going to need to *sink* a lot of money into it."

Smart real estate investors don't *sink* money into anything. They make shrewd *capital investments*. And I'd argue that the first step in proving that you understand the crucial difference lies in using the proper verbiage. The titanic sank. Naive investors *sink* their money into unworthy properties. Smart ones invest in properties that show promise, thereby transforming tired eyesores into stunning properties that people will enter into a bidding war to try and purchase.

It also stands to reason that in order to make capital investments, you need to have a steady cash flow. As I've previously mentioned, I was the originator of the first no-money-down programs in Canada in the mid-1990s—all while building a multimillion-dollar-a-year renovation business at the same time.

Over time the ways in which real estate investors build up cash reserves have changed, even if the basic tenets have remained pretty much the same.

While the best overall strategy, over the last twenty years, has been to view real estate holdings as a long-term investment, there comes a time when you need to turn over your capital to ensure a steady cash flow.

Let me give you a very simple real-world example to illustrate this principle in action.

One of my earliest personal residences was a townhome on Benson Avenue in Richmond Hill, which I'd acquired from my father and one of his business partners. In order to maximize its value, I followed the very same checklist and advice I've offered to you in this chapter.

I financed it in a creative way. I used leverage to purchase it, putting down very little of my own money. I immediately made a capital improvement to my basement, renting out a portion of it to a friend. I also turned my garage into a makeshift storage unit, leasing it out to bring in additional income. When all was said and done, the rent and storage checks that I collected covered my mortgage with plenty of money left over for me to enjoy.

As a result of this excess cash flow, I was able to purchase a few lots on a property just north of my home at 96 Leyburn Avenue. I sold the corner of Leyburn and Stancroft to my father, which was one parcel. But then he transformed it into three parcels of which I bought one and my mother and uncle bought the other two. But I didn't stop there: I continued to assemble properties in the Benson area, which was, at that time, a transitional area. I did so by leveraging financing, which led to significant midsized developments and eventually a change of use that produced high-end townhomes.

I built my first single-family home on a lot at 96 Leyburn Avenue, staying disciplined and true to my checklist. But consider the financial benefits of this move. Having moved out of my Benson property, I could now rent both its upper and lower floors, boosting my rental income while I enjoyed the perks of living in my new home.

When the value of my new home rose precipitously, I immediately sold it, pocketing the commission myself, to generate extra cash flow and make a profit.

When I moved back into my townhome on Benson, I avoided the temptation of taking over extra space from my renters to re-create how much space I had previously enjoyed in my single-family home. Instead, I decided to keep renting out all of the remaining units and lease storage space in my garage.

While it's true that holding on to my property on Leyburn for a few extra years might have generated a substantial return, I could now take those profits and immediately invest them in another, more expensive property with an even larger potential upside.

I can't stress the following point enough: as a real estate investor, you don't ever want to have your cash flow directly tied to your equity. Try doing what I did: improve your cash flow via timely real estate sales, smart renovations, and management fees. In this way you grow your equity, while reserving the ability to recycle it through the system, as you watch it grow again and again.

> **You don't ever want to have your cash flow directly tied to your equity.**

Continuing to work as a buyer's agent will provide you the safety net needed to take on these kinds of risks.

But I'd be remiss if I didn't end our discussion by focusing on the human element of real estate investing. When you run a successful buyer's program, you'll develop trusted financing contacts. And you will become an invaluable referral source for lenders. These connections are extremely valuable because they create additional opportunities to help you finance your own projects.

If you've proven yourself to lenders—by staying true to your word—those same lenders will go to bat for you when you need quick capital. In fact, when your financing contacts make a recommendation for approval, they will often write it in their notes that you're a trusted referral source.

A word of warning, however: not all lenders can be trusted. I've certainly learned the dangers of putting all your eggs in one basket when it comes to borrowing from overextended lenders. All of us, at one time or another, can get caught in a bad deal. So ensure your financing sources know how to play the game as well as you do—and make sure they're the kinds of lenders who know where to draw the line.

As I've noted, bank lenders and financing institutions can be a very hypocritical lot—and very cycle oriented. You can be cruising along, doing everything right, and then somebody, through no fault of your own, can develop a different agenda and pull the plug on you.

As an investor forge relationships with different kinds of people. By doing so you can become a connector who brings diverse people together.

Make it a priority to follow through on your promises, and do your best to make people make money in the process.

At the end of the day, making it happen for buyers, investors, and lenders is a necessity, as each successful deal allows you to burnish your reputation and improve your portfolio.

Case in point: After I moved back to my townhome on Benson Avenue, I improved my gains by working with a new set of partners and assembling a new site. I focused on changing the use of a property on 129 and 121 Hall Street in Richmond Hill.

The frontage on these two properties, which were basically teardowns, measured approximately 151 feet wide and 190 feet deep. I acquired these parcels with my uncle Anthony, a trusted partner in our renovation business.

We'd already built a number of homes together and completed a few "top ups," ripping the roofs off old bungalows and transforming them into four-story homes. We were ready to take the next step and tackle a midsize development.

We followed the same game plan as before, albeit on a larger scale. We'd acquire old homes, leverage them, rent them out, and then go about renovating and developing the overall site. We financed our development costs through our renovation business, which I'd been able to grow with the proceeds accrued from my buyer's program.

This new site included zoning allowances that allowed for more intensified build-outs. It was located just around the corner from the townhomes on Benson Avenue. Only there was a key difference between the two sites.

Like most infill developments, each townhome on Benson came with its own private driveway, which connected to an adjoining street. Given how much space these driveways covered, there was only enough room for a total of seven townhomes to be built on the site.

In our new parcel, we were free to build underground parking, provided it offered at least one direct-access path to the street. This more efficient use of the land allowed us to build twenty-four townhomes, complete with underground parking and an inner courtyard.

Through it all we kept our costs in check and preserved our cash flow. In time we brought on another construction partner, thereby reducing our overall capital investment. My expertise was in the land, so I focused on development approvals, while my uncle and business partner, Sam, handled the construction. This divide-and-conquer strategy enabled us to utilize our individual strengths and finish the work as efficiently as possible.

This far more dense and utilitarian design leaned into my belief in new urbanism, which proved to be not only lucrative but also years ahead of its time.

I share this story to remind you that you can't afford to remain static. When you're building a real estate portfolio, you can begin by tackling modest projects, but you must continually push yourself to take on more ambitious developments as you progress. Once you begin to feel comfortable, reject the voice in your head that says, "This is good enough."

Know that there are greater thrills and more substantial rewards awaiting those who seek out new opportunities and take on greater risks.

Anyone who accepts the challenge of developing an entire parcel themselves—acquiring the land, overseeing the approval plan for the site, and then managing marketing needs, financing, final build-outs, and sales—will reap extraordinary experience and unexpected financial rewards.

The key, as I noted earlier, is to remember that we all, at one time or another, need to turn our capital over for cash-flow purposes and build additional equity. This twenty-four-townhome site on Hill Street, which we dubbed the Manors of Mill Pond, generated millions of dollars and represented a substantial step up for me in my evolution as a real estate investor.

And true to the cycle of things, the partnerships and connections that I forged allowed me to take on bigger projects, just as you will too. Remember that rock-solid real estate portfolios aren't built in a day. They simply gain heft and strength, like a snowball rolling down the hill, over time. The key is to stay disciplined and remember the following key takeaways:

Working in different markets will enable you to help renters become homeowners and existing homeowners to find their dream homes. This time-consuming work on behalf of buyers will aid you in identifying opportunities in affordable areas and help you in diversifying your portfolio.

- Generate a plan that ensures you make money the minute you take ownership of a property. Devise a financing strategy, long before you make a purchase, and then continue to use that blueprint to wisely borrow and deploy capital. View every improvement as an investment by remaining laser focused on changing the use of the site or building and maintaining your own elevated standards of quality.

- Never allow your available cash flow to remain tied up in your equity. In order to create real wealth, you won't be able to cash in on a single huge win, kick your feet up, and expect those proceeds to carry you all the way through the next buy-and-sell cycle. You need to build your business around a steady influx of cash to ensure your wealth continually grows.

- When opportunities arise, you may have to turn your capital over to take advantage of market conditions. Try to generate money from cash-flow generators tied to your existing investments, including commissions and management fees, which can then be recycled into other future properties.

- Be a connector: do your best to bring people together, and always make good on your promises. Work with trustworthy investors, buyers, and partners. And be a solid referral source to mortgage specialists. This goodwill will create opportunities for you to finance your own projects.

- In time new participants will evolve into loyal partners, who will then help you take on additional investment opportunities. Thus when you find a deal that you *need* to immediately act on, all you'll need to do is pick up the phone, and trustworthy partners, clients, and investors will jump at the chance to follow your lead.

CHAPTER 4

THE NEW CONSTRUCTION PARADOX:
THERE'S ALWAYS BETTER VALUE IN RESALE

I t's time to address the big, hulking elephant in the room—that is, the lingering debate over whether new real estate agents should focus on new construction or work with existing properties.

Now, more than ever before, brokers seem intent on using new-homebuilder programs as recruiting tools to attract new talent. And for good reason. Buyers have always been drawn to turnkey elegance. They want instant gratification. The glamour and enchantment of the new. New buildings. New homes. New condos. All packed with designer kitchens, spacious bathrooms, and chic new accoutrements.

There's a certain *je ne sais quoi* to buying something that's new, isn't there? It doesn't matter if it costs more and offers less long-term value. None of that seems to enter into the equation for some buyers, who are willing to pay extra for the novelty of guaranteed glitter and shine.

And that's understandable. As a builder and developer myself, I understand the allure of new construction. Which is why, at TREC, we have our own proprietary "new homebuilder" program.

Our platform is structured differently than most, as we are extraordinarily selective about the new developments we recommend to our clients. We work exclusively with reputable builders who've earned our trust as well as developers who've built a reputation for performing quality work and honoring their down payments. As such, we view our new homebuilder program as a value-added benefit for our clients, not the primary driver of our practice.

Occasionally, a young real estate agent will want to know why that's the case—why we spend so much time helping buyers sift through existing inventories, while others are so obsessed with pushing their agents to chase new developments and new construction.

The answer, of course, is that most brokerages don't want to take the time, or shoulder the expenses, to teach young agents how to properly assess the value of existing property and how to respectfully haggle with a seller to obtain a better deal for their clients. When it comes to resale, a property is ultimately worth whatever someone is willing to pay for it. Timing is critical, as is one's ability to make a strong argument as to why someone should reduce their asking price.

In the early- to mid-2000s, an investor friend of mine and I acquired a site at 2464 Weston Road. The parcel was composed of two old homes set on a large lot backing into the Humber River. This site ended up being my first large-scale development, which I will elaborate on in later chapters.

To make a long story short, the property was originally listed at $2.5 million. My partner and I negotiated a purchase price of $1.5 million with a 180 conditional due-diligence period, which enabled us time to negotiate a development proposal with the city of Toronto. Prior to waiving the conditions and firming up on the purchase, we outlined to the seller all the obstacles and challenges of this particular zoning approval along with all the technical challenges that we'd face as developers. We managed to negotiate a further $500,000 reduction off the original purchase price from $1.5 million to $1 million.

The major takeaway? Here was a property originally listed for $2.5 million, but thanks to our tenacity and negotiations, we managed to convince the seller to reduce the final purchase price to $1 million.

Working with existing buildings and investing in the right neighborhoods is hard work, which is why so many novice agents are drawn to new builds, where prices are more static.

While I think it's important for brokerages to offer clients the opportunity to buy into new construction properties, it's also vital for newly minted agents to remember that all the top-producing real estate agents specialize in resale. Resale is where the money is made in terms of sales and real wealth creation.

Although I've mentioned this before, it bears repeating: there's always more long-term value in buying and investing in existing properties than in new construction.

Most real estate agents understand this intrinsically, even if they're still drawn to the shiny new object du jour. Which is why, whenever a young doe-eyed real estate agent asks me to elaborate, I sit them down and tell them the story of the Toronto SkyDome.

> **There's always more long-term value in buying and investing in existing properties than in new construction.**

Today, the SkyDome, which is home to the Toronto Blue Jays, is called the Rogers Centre. But back in the late 1980s, when plans were still being ironed out, it was heralded as the last great engineering marvel of the twentieth century.

In some ways all that hyperbole was justified, as the SkyDome has earned a place in the history books for being the first professional sports stadium to feature a fully retractable roof.

It's often been suggested that the origin story of the SkyDome should begin with the disastrous 1982 Grey Cup, when an ill-timed second-half storm not only sent fans scurrying for shelter but also arguably cost the Toronto Argonauts a chance to win the Canadian Football League championship.

One of the spectators ducking for cover that day happened to be Metropolitan Toronto chairman Paul Godfrey, who viewed the devastating Grey Cup fiasco as an opportunity to rally public support for the construction of a brand-new, state-of-the-art domed stadium.

Godfrey's impassioned pitch set the public's imagination ablaze with excitement. Soon studies were being commissioned around greater Toronto to pinpoint the best site for the project. Just as one might expect, heated debates soon erupted as to where exactly the stadium should be built (as well as how much private money should be allocated for its construction).

By the time a site was formally chosen (near the CN Tower in Toronto) and construction commenced in 1986, the project's total price tag had ballooned from an estimated $130 million to $242 million.[1] Any concerns over these rising costs, however, took a back seat to the public's excitement over early renderings and blueprints.

Who, after all, possessed the courage to decry budget overruns and the lack of long-term ROI when Toronto's new stadium promised every bell and whistle one could ever dream of?

Local reporters, in a preview of how everyone now promotes new construction projects, couldn't find enough ink to spill about the place. The SkyDome, the newspapers proclaimed, would be a modern-day Colosseum. Its curved 110-metric-ton roof, which arched 282 feet in the air, would be tall enough to house a thirty-one-story

---

1   Jamie Bradburn, "Historicist: The Road to SkyDome," Torontoist, June 13, 2009, https://torontoist.com/2009/06/historicist_the_road_to_skydome/.

building. And the stadium's huge new scoreboard, projected to be the largest in the world, would stretch four stories high and boast 420,000 individual lights.[2]

The SkyDome's much-ballyhooed screen, some argued, would succeed in putting the word "jumbo" back in jumbotron. And then, of course, there was the allure of so many glitzy new amenities: new restaurants inside the park plus new fitness clubs and an attached hotel boasting rooms that directly overlooked the field.

You would have been hard pressed, back in the 1980s, to find anyone who didn't want a piece of this massive development. But, like so many other high-profile projects, the math grew increasingly vexing with every passing year.

This wasn't, after all, a retrofit of an existing arena. This was a brand-new sports cathedral. By the time the SkyDome made its rather inauspicious debut in 1989—the skies opened up that day and dumped buckets of rain on the festivities—construction costs had gone stratospheric, totaling $570 million.[3]

Less than four years later, the thrill of Toronto enjoying a new stadium was replaced by the reality of its onerous debt load, which hovered around $400 million.[4] No one had bothered to crunch the numbers and realize that it was now virtually impossible for the SkyDome to turn a profit.

As a result local officials decided to sell the SkyDome to a private consortium of investors for $151 million in 1994.[5] Four years later, in 1998, the venue was sold again, this time for just $98 million. By 2004

2   PBS, "Wonders of the World: SkyDome," accessed February 7, 2023, https://www.pbs.org/wgbh/buildingbig/wonder/structure/sky.html.

3   Bradburn, "Historicist."

4   CBC News, "You Win Some, You Lose Some," February 9, 2011, https://www.cbc.ca/news/canada/you-win-some-you-lose-some-1.1060052.

5   CBC News, "You Win Some."

the Blue Jays organization itself decided prices had sunk so low that the team couldn't resist snatching it up for just $25 million,[6] a sales price that represented an embarrassing fraction of its original construction costs.

So I ask you: Who got the best deal?

Answer: the Blue Jays, who understood the power of resale buying.

My point, of course, is that there's money to be made by developing and investing in new builds, but the quickest and most dependable way to generate real wealth is by focusing on resale opportunities, whether you're an agent or an investor.

One of my primary aims in writing this book is to ensure that everyone, especially new real estate agents, understands this fundamental but often overlooked fact. It bothers me to see so many talented people excitedly join our industry, only to watch their careers get derailed by get-rich-quick schemes and false promises.

For, in many cases, it's not a lack of intelligence or grit that derails new real estate agents. They simply start their journey off on the wrong foot by hitching their wagons to the inexperienced brokerage house and devoting too much time to new construction, when they could learn—and earn—twice as much by simply avoiding both of these pitfalls.

My advice: if a pitch about a new development or a broker's new homebuilder program sounds too good to be true—too fun, too easy, too much of a sure thing—chances are it is.

In this business there are no express elevators that will shuttle you straight to the penthouse. The key is to embrace every training opportunity that comes your way. Attend every broker-supported Zoom meeting. Take educational courses. And devote as much time as possible to sitting at the feet of those who've done well, both in terms of building their own real estate portfolio and helping clients build theirs too.

---

6   CBC News, "Blue Jays Buying SkyDome for $25M," November 29, 2004, https://www.cbc.ca/news/business/blue-jays-buying-skydome-for-25m-1.495992.

To this day I still attend as many training seminars as I can. And I make it a point to keep in contact with trusted mentors and seek out new ideas from industry professionals, both inside and outside of our own brokerage.

One of the best things you can do as a young agent, as I'll demonstrate in subsequent chapters, is to build a strong database and provide all your clients with exceptional service. Generate a robust client-engagement plan, and then follow through on it.

So don't be mesmerized by brokerages that promise you the world if you focus on new builds, as that very narrow path will box you in and reduce your chances of long-term success.

It's important to remember that new-construction developers always operate on a cost approach. Every project begins with a careful evaluation of the cost of the land and potential construction costs. Developers must take into account overhead and the size of their interest payments. And after that's been completed, they must establish how much of a profit they hope to make once their building or the last of their units is sold.

In order to bolster the odds that they'll earn that predetermined payout, they have to set a hard price for each unit and stick with that price.

Developers don't like to negotiate—or, in the very least, aren't in the habit of doing so willingly. When they establish a sales price, they lock it in place. So while your heart might flutter at the thought of walking buyers through shiny new buildings with trendy amenities, consider the amount of time it'll take you to actually earn your commission.

How are you going to stay cash-flow positive during the eighteen months or more needed for the project to get off the ground? Not to mention the additional eighteen months or more required for the building to be fully built.

Based on that timetable, you're unlikely to see your commission for three or four years. Developers may offer an advance in the short term; however, you'll have to wait for the majority of your commission to come much later. And if a project doesn't actually get built, you can bet that most developers have included claw-back clauses in their contracts, which allow them to obtain their advances back.

So why focus all your time on new construction when you can show buyers existing properties with good bones and even better potential, all while earning your commission in as little as sixty days?

Besides, many novice agents assume that if they simply recommend a new build to buyers, and they go on to make a purchase, that they're guaranteed a commission. Not so. While this is often the case, remember that builders tend to be shrewd businesspeople. They understand that there's no hard-and-fast definition as to what qualifies as a formal "introduction" to a site.

If you, as a buyer's agent, don't escort your clients onto the site or into its sales headquarters and personally sign a form that documents your representation, there's nothing stopping a developer from swooping in and taking the commission for themselves.

After all, it's not unusual for buyers to visit a site on their own, even if you were the one who suggested they should see it in the first place. When buyers travel to a site without you and sign on the dotted line, developers can claim that sale, leaving you with nothing.

I recommend you stay away from builders who show any reticence in working with brokers. For me that's always a serious red flag, which increases the chances you will run into trouble down the line. If a developer stops cooperating with you—which often happens after they get their financing conditions satisfied—don't bother trying to win them over. They've likely moved on already, as they've devised a way to maximize their profits.

This isn't a knock, in any way, shape, or form, on developers. I'm a developer myself. Truth is, if we can find a way to save money, we will. As buyers and sellers, as agents and developers, we're all searching for ways to maximize our returns. Which is why the key for you, as an agent, is to stay focused on the real prize, which you'll invariably find with more regularity in the resale market.

Long-term success in our business is a direct result of developing a good reputation and providing your clients sound advice. If you have a buyer's best interests in mind, it's incumbent upon you to inform them that their initial deposits could be tied up for years—and that some projects may never get built at all.

There are other risks worth discussing as well. If market conditions shift or prices jump, some developers will try to terminate all existing contracts to ensure they rake in more cash. So I implore you: be honest with your clients and educate them about these risks. Reinforce the truism that nothing is guaranteed and that most new-home warranties will only protect them up to $60,000.

It comes down to this: if you are going to sell a new build, make sure you're dealing with reputable builders.

If your client falls in love with a new build, and you've outlined all the potential risks and costs—please make sure to discuss the hidden costs of potential add-ons within a unit or house—and they remain committed to moving forward, then by all means support them. Get your buyer's agreement signed, and do everything in your power to get them quickly moved into their dream unit.

Just know that the more responsible thing to do, in my opinion, is to educate them about the compounding value of buying and developing existing properties. Some brokerages specialize in new home sites. And in some cases, that's all they do. That's perfectly fine, but I'd argue that focusing on new builds is rarely where you want to start your career.

When you focus on new construction, you're dependent on people coming to you. If a project fails to gain sufficient traction or foot traffic, you're out of luck. Simply put, new construction is a more retail-oriented business.

Whereas if you focus more on existing properties, you can generate your own good fortune. You can work as much as your schedule allows. You can put in all the legwork required to acquire new listings. You can talk to clients over the phone when they really need you. You can field questions that will impact their lives in profound ways. And you can leverage your creativity with financing solutions that will allow you to build substantial wealth at a phenomenally rapid clip.

By doing all of the above, you'll develop a reputation as a real problem solver. In short you'll learn how to run, when the new construction folks are sitting peacefully in their offices, waiting for the action to come to them.

If anything, I've always felt I was doing my clients a disservice if I didn't remind them, time and again, that the three most important words in real estate will always be *location, location, location.*

As I've already stressed, I'm not a green field developer. My whole business is focused on infill development and intensifying and revital-izing properties in inner cities. I believe in respectfully beautifying and redeveloping our urban areas. But I also recognize that everyone is in favor of intensification, except when it happens to occur in their own backyard. However, the rewards of battling through the approval process—not to mention the sweat and heartache that one invests into resale investments—can far outweigh the comforts of a new build from a wealth-creation standpoint. Renovating and retrofitting a property or custom building your own home on an infill lot in an already established community is the right business strategy, as resale opportunities far outweigh cookie-cutter new development opportu-nities, where the only increase in value is appreciation.

Case in point: In 1998 I bought a one-and-a-half-acre infill lot for $225,000 in Richmond Hill, an established community that has now blossomed into a "new urban center." As opposed to buying a brand-new house in a cookie-cutter subdivision development, I chose to develop what I believed would evolve into a very valuable plot of land. It didn't matter to me that it was located in a flood zone or that it was overrun with trees; I could see its potential the day I walked its grounds.

The rewards of battling through the approval process— not to mention the sweat and heartache that one invests into resale investments— can far outweigh the comforts of a new build from a wealth-creation standpoint.

If anything, the overly wooded area allowed me to establish the footprint of my house about two hundred feet from a nearby road, thus giving me that rarest of benefits: true solitude.

Slowly, I began to build my dream home on that site. I made the sacrifices and spent the money needed to do it right, when I could have easily bought a new home in a subdivision and sat back and enjoyed the finished project.

I hired an architect, secured private financing, and built it. By September of 2000, my house was roughly 70 percent completed. In terms of costs, I'd already invested somewhere in the ballpark of $600,000 above my acquisition costs, but I didn't stop there. I continued, year after year, making targeted improvements.

When I initially moved in, I was single, so I rented an upstairs bedroom to a friend, rented out another portion of the house to a couple, and then rented out the basement to another tenant. What can I say, other than the fact that I inherited a capacity to be very frugal from my mother?

A glamorous start? Far from it. Here I was, living in a huge home in a beautiful area, but inhabiting only a meager sliver of it. To some people this might sound like an odd decision, but I was committed to following through on my long-term plan.

On occasion some of my friends would tap me on my shoulder and say, "Hey, Dean, you realize you could be living in that gorgeous new subdivision right down the road for the same amount of money you've invested in your house, don't you?"

Of course I did. But I also understood a few fundamental truths about real estate investing, namely that when you buy new construction, you're essentially painting yourself into a corner. You're not buying land that can be developed for future use, nor are you giving yourself substantial opportunities to grow. In essence you're trading future potential for present-day comforts.

So I kept building. *Building. Building. Building.* I made improvements, some small, others larger, over a twenty-year period. One year I oversaw some landscaping improvements around the house. Another year I made a capital investment in a better sewer system. In 2015 I expanded the size of the house, adding a major addition to the upstairs of my home and extending another over my garage.

Now, my home is a 5,200-square-foot beauty boasting five bedrooms plus an ice rink and basketball court in the back. The point, of course, is that it took time, sweat equity, and personal sacrifices to make that all happen. Similar to the way a new real estate agent is forced to choose between the easy "new build" path and the more winding one that requires vision, creativity, sacrifice, execution, and sticking power, I chose the latter and was rewarded for it more and more with each passing year.

My house grew along with my personal wealth. And today you can't find a parcel of land like mine anywhere near Richmond Hill. Why? Because as other new developments were erected, the lot sizes for those who wanted to move in began to shrink all around them.

I'm confident that the homeowners who bought into those new developments did well for themselves. But they certainly won't be able to match the overall return on their investments that I'll be able to enjoy as the years roll by.

With every passing year, my land has grown exponentially in value. Today, it's impossible to find a 1.5-acre lot anywhere near Toronto. Which, of course, is my point. Anyone can buy new. And any real estate agent can represent buyers looking for the next shiny new development. But why settle for an average return, when you can put yourself in a position to achieve something special?

I'd estimate that my land alone in this spot is now worth more than $2.5 million. Tack on the value of my home, and I'd wager that the entire parcel is worth at least $5 million to $6 million, perhaps even millions more should a smart and motivated buyer come along. Add in the fact that this is my principal residence, which means the profit I accrue is not taxed in Canada, and you understand the magnitude of that gain. It's not a bad return when factoring in the cost of land combined with construction cost is under $1.2 million.

Nevertheless, I hope to redevelop my property further, by working with two of my neighbors on a project that has the potential to deliver a payout worth triple what our land and house are currently worth by changing their use into an intensified built development of high-end executive townhomes.

Only time will tell whether we succeed, but one thing is certain. We are willing to take the more arduous path to enjoy greater rewards. The question, of course, is whether you are willing to do the same.

CHAPTER 5

CHANGE CAN BE REALLY GOOD:
CHANGE THE USE FOR THE MOST PRODIGIOUS GAINS

If I were to invite you to grab a seat in a large conference room—with nothing in it but a few empty seats and a huge dry-erase board with a marker Velcroed to its corner—and ask you to play a simple word-association game, would you be up for the challenge?

Let's say I ask you to close your eyes for a moment while I write a word on the board. When I give you the signal, you're to open your eyes, read the word, and tell me the first thing that flits and flickers to mind.

Let's try it.

Imagine you've sealed your eyelids shut, listened to me squeak a marker along the board. I tell you to open your eyes, and you see the phrase *change of use* printed on the board.

Your mind immediately races where?

There are no wrong answers here. Whatever pops into your head is fine.

You see the words "change of use," and you think what?

A garden apartment? A fulfillment center? A towering office building? Do you see renters living in a cozy little basement unit, complete with a small kitchen and cramped bathroom? Or an old '80s-era mall being razed to the ground to make room for a gleaming new suburban subdivision?

I bet you weren't thinking about parking, though, were you? Parking spots? And parking lots? Or that sexiest of topics: mutual access easement agreements?

But maybe you should be, though. Because, over the years, I've found there are extraordinary profits to be made by focusing on the small stuff, especially the granular improvements that can immediately bolster the value of a piece of land.

Truth is most budding investors and developers these days don't give much thought to the small stuff. But if you stick around long enough, some of your greatest gains will come from scouring urban areas for change-of-use projects.

My definition of the term "change of use" goes something like this: think of it as any instance in which you purchase a property in its current form and legally change some aspect of how the property functions.

Your goal for any change-of-use project is to increase the value of your property *twice*: first, by making the initial change to the building and then again, over an extended period of time, when the value of that change is formally realized.

I recognize that there's nothing innately exciting about analyzing the financial potential of an old parking lot. Or deploying your hard-earned capital to hire consultants to study noise pollution and run studies analyzing how the shadow of a new building might impact neighboring properties or impact traffic. Or, truth be told, mapping out how to deliver an impressive presentation before local urban planning commissioners and land tribunals.

But I'd argue it's precisely these skills that end up being the difference between an investment that yields a decent profit and a gargantuan one.

Stay with me here because, as I've already stressed—and this is worth bolding—your greatest gains in real estate invariably come by changing the use of existing properties that everyone else has overlooked.

And to drive that point home, I want to tell you a story about one of the oddest-looking parking lots I've been lucky enough to own.

Let me paint you a picture of the scene. Slip back in time with me to the year 2006, long before anyone ever connected the words "great" and "financial crisis" together in the same sentence.

> **Your greatest gains in real estate invariably come by changing the use of existing properties that everyone else has overlooked.**

Imagine a rather pedestrian-looking corner parcel on Caledonia Road and Eglinton Avenue in Toronto's Briar Hill neighborhood. It's definitely not the most desirable place to live. Developers speed right past it, every single day of the week, without giving it a second thought.

But context is critical here. Real estate prices across the greater Toronto area were soaring at the time, which meant everyone's attention was focused on all the usual places: Bridle Path. Forest Hill South. Casa Loma.

Everyone, that is, except me, because I'd become smitten with a rather odd-looking corner parcel, in the city of York, which is now officially part of Toronto's "mega city."

I'd called a Realtor to learn more about a different site I'd been researching. But as we began to talk, he asked if I'd be interested in an exclusive listing he'd just acquired on Eglinton and Caledonia.

This parcel, which was owned by a local physician, included five different buildings. There were three old brick bungalows, two of which the doctor used for office space, a commercial building housing a restaurant and a few residential units perched on its second floor, and a rather strange-looking triangular-shaped building that was being used as a pharmacy.

The seller was pitching the lot as a "can't-miss" redevelopment opportunity. As an added bonus, existing approvals had already been authorized for the construction of a six-story medical building on the site.

The downside? The ownership history of this particular parcel was a bit complicated. The lot's current owner, who we'll refer to as Dr. C, had previously sold it to a buyer before taking it back via a foreclosure sale. The good doctor had taken out a mortgage on the property but felt this was an ideal time to sell it.

His asking price? $1.3 million.

The parcel did not come with A-rated buildings and tenants. But for years rumors swirled that the Toronto Transit Commission might be interested in adding a subway station somewhere nearby.

Although this remained nothing more than idle gossip at the time, I became so convinced that these rumors were bound to become a reality, as the recent population boom felt across Toronto would surely necessitate the addition of more subway stops radiating outward from the city center.

My goal was to buy into the neighborhood sooner rather than later, as I could foresee a future in which a subway expansion in the area might send prices skyrocketing.

After performing my research, I negotiated an agreement to purchase the parcel for $1.2 million, which was conditional on a ninety-day due-diligence period.

The owner and seller's agent had assumed, without actually doing a title search, that all five parcels had been legally merged into one lot, which is what you'd expect when parcels like these were all owned by one party.

But I couldn't be certain that was actually the case until I pulled the survey and the plans, as I'd run into a similar problem on a different parcel.

When I obtained the files, I quickly dialed my real estate lawyer. I asked him if he was seeing what I was seeing.

Indeed, he was. All five parcels were still *separate*.

Nothing had been merged. There were some scattered parking spaces and an asphalt parking lot, but the spaces weren't *legal* parking spaces.

To make matters worse, neither the ingress nor the egress leading to those parking spots had been legally formalized. They weren't on any title or survey, and the owner had never requested that they become legal via a committee of adjustment submission.

I was staring at something that we refer to in the business as a "dog's breakfast," which roughly translated means a complete and total mess.

Nevertheless, I could envision this corner lot becoming a real long-term wealth generator, as long as I played my cards right.

I needed to secure a mutual easement agreement that allowed all five parcels to *share* these parking spots. If I could also legalize the ingress and egress along Caledonia that led to the parking lot, I was very confident that the value of every one of my parcels would rise exponentially.

The doctor had set a $1.3 million asking price in the belief that someone would swoop in, purchase it, and immediately start constructing a medical building on the site.

But that got me thinking: What if I didn't redevelop the land at all? What if I simply changed the use of the parcel by legalizing the parking spaces that were already there—as well as the ingress and egress to the parking lot—by securing a mutual easement, which would allow all five properties to use those parking spots?

I immediately hired a traffic consultant to help me to do just that through the city's committee of adjustment. Then, I phoned an investor friend of mine.

One look at the survey and he agreed to write me a check for $250,000 to cover closing costs and other expenses. Given that this was a man who was often slow to invest money in a deal without his solicitor's approval, I knew I was onto something potentially big here.

From there I decided to visit with the parcel's owner a second time and negotiate a reduction in price.

Remember: just because you've tied something up at one price doesn't mean you have to purchase it for that original amount.

I informed the seller that there were clear title issues in play here. "Your parking lots," I told him with blunt candor, "are not legal parking lots. This is a mess. Any appraiser and any bank will immediately raise all sorts of red flags the minute they inspect the property or request a survey."

I hoped I could attain an easement, but what if I didn't succeed in that endeavor? After all, I was currently staring at a five-parcel lot bordering dozens of *illegal* parking spots.

Recognizing this newfound risk, the doctor agreed to lower his selling price to $1.1 million. I told him that I'd accept his offer, provided we entered into a vendor take-back agreement for a period of exactly one year. And to my relief, he accepted.

A vendor take-back, or VTB mortgage, is an agreement in which the seller lends a buyer funds to purchase their own property. In essence the seller acts as a de facto mortgage lender, providing the buyer sufficient capital to complete the sale. In return the buyer agrees to make regular interest payments until the loan is paid off.

As far as I was concerned, my proposal amounted to a win-win for everyone involved. I could use a portion of the $250,000 I borrowed from my investor as a down payment to purchase the property. Meanwhile, Dr. C, who would rake in more than a million dollars from the sale alone, could sit back and collect 8 percent interest from me over the next year on the $800,000 VTB deal we'd worked out between us.

That same year we were granted the mutual easement and change-of-use approvals for all the parking spots for all five parcels. The city of Toronto was more than happy to approve them because I'd taken the time and expense to legalize something that had been illegal in the past.

Once the easement was approved, I attained separate mortgages for each of the parcels. Each of the three bungalows was appraised at $400,000, equaling $1.2 million. In addition, the triangular pharmacy and the third building were appraised for a total of $1.3 million, elevating the overall value of all five parcels to $2.5 million.

Within the course of just twelve months, I'd made a $1.4 million profit simply by *changing the use* of those illegal parking spots. I was able to obtain five separate mortgages on five separate parcels with a legalized parking arrangement. This allowed me to refinance all of our money out and the cash flow from the properties carried all the expenses.

And just as I predicted, approval for a gleaming new subway station was granted for development just down the street from my site. Over the years investors have offered me in excess of $10 million to buy that parcel, but I've politely declined every offer because I see massive long-term potential in the site.

I can envision a new building being built there in the future. It'll be another change-of-use project, of course: a towering residential building. I see intensity and density. And a long-term ROI that puts even my initial gains to shame.

One of the key takeaways to be gleaned from this story, of course, is that most young real estate investors don't associate the term "change of use" with parking. They immediately see high-rise apartment buildings or green fields being transformed into subdivisions.

But savvy real estate investors understand that small, seemingly inconsequential changes can generate major short-term and long-term profits. Remember: in the real estate world, you don't just want to make money when you sell. You need to make money the moment you purchase a property.

To do so you have to train your mind to see what a property is likely to become over time. You'd be shocked how few developers and investors possess this extraordinarily important skill set.

So don't be frivolous. Just because you happen to have the available cash to buy into an area that everyone else is clamoring to get into, ask yourself this essential question: Is there a potential change of use in play, perhaps in a different neighborhood just down the road, that will cost you a fraction of the same price?

Can you develop a site that can just as easily (and quickly) generate a massive profit over both the short and long term?

If so, always go with the latter.

How to Be a Better "People" Person

A quick reminder of something I've mentioned before: I don't care what anyone tells you, real estate is a people-centric business. I worked hard to earn Dr. C's trust the first time we shook hands, and I went out of my way to reinforce that relationship every day thereafter. I personally delivered every one of my checks to his front door every month, often spending hours chatting with him in his living room after every drop-off.

I encourage all budding real estate investors to study change-of-use projects like the one I've just outlined, because they force you to develop the type of interpersonal skills that distinguish good investors from great ones.

Make it a priority, for instance, to build a rapport with listing agents. Analyze overlooked neighborhoods. Be fearless in negotiating—and then renegotiating—with owners and municipal review boards. Do your best to play both the long and short game simultaneously.

In short, follow through on your plans.

But one thing is undeniable: in order to execute, you need to be able to navigate the political labyrinth that is local government. A word of warning: you can't afford to ignore the plans and proclivities of city politicians. You can't ignore the amount of weight and influence that city planners can throw around either. Nor can you overestimate the importance of ensuring your local planning committee supports your project.

In short, whenever you advocate for a rezoning project or a change of use, you need to do everything in your power to obtain a positive planning report from your local city or town.

Case in point: Early in my career, when I was still in my thirties, I assembled four wonderful parcels on the corner of Benson and Hall in Richmond Hill. My intention was to develop a beautiful thirty-eight-stack townhouse on the site, complete with an underground parking lot.

It was the kind of project, in all honesty, that was light-years ahead of its time. The only problem? The planning department and local politicians wanted to see more traditional design elements and structures on the site. And of course, local residents rushed in to complain to their representatives that they didn't want any changes at all.

It didn't matter one iota to the planning commissioner that we presented unimpeachable arguments as to why our intensified build form made perfect sense, not only in terms of its utility but its design sense as well. At the end of the day, the city didn't like the project as we'd designed it. And that was that.

Only I couldn't let it go. Being young (and perhaps a little too stubborn), I decided to fight the powers that be. Suffice to say things didn't go well for me as a result. Looking back, the first phrase that comes to mind is "humbling experience."

In Toronto we used to have a tribunal known as the Ontario Municipal Board, or OMB for short. Today, it's called the Ontario Land Tribunal, which I mentioned previously. When I was in my thirties, I felt I could present a compelling argument to the OMB as to why the density of our specific blueprints was smart urban planning.

So I riffled around my piggy bank and lawyered up—unaware that I'd essentially committed myself to burning through an ungodly amount of money in pursuit of a no-win cause. I lost the case due to a technicality regarding where we'd placed the access routes on our blueprints. I probably could have won the case had I changed the access route and compromised a little, but I didn't, and it cost me big time.

The commissioner of planning at the time not only dug her heels in during the public meetings, but she also decided to make an example out of me. She dressed me down with such force that a local resident came up to me after the meeting and whispered, "What exactly did you do to get her so riled up?"

I learned a powerful albeit expensive lesson that year: never, ever squander hundreds of thousands of dollars to fight your local planning commissioner thinking you can just shoehorn in a development proposal by lawyering up and bulldozing your way through. You must always try and find a way to get them onside. A positive planning report from the city is essential. Developers simply can't overcome the political pressures that politicians encounter when NIMBY (not in my backyard) residents come out in force to oppose a project.

No matter how sophisticated your plan may look on paper, it's going to be an uphill battle if you are going against the city planners or a negative planning report from the city. Your chances of success are slim. You can't always solve the political challenges; all you can do is good urban planning, and that's the mindset for success.

But I suppose if there's a silver lining to the story, it's that I learned how to temporarily shelve my defiance and negotiate a profitable compromise.

After being harangued by the commissioner, I offered a *mea culpa* to the OMB. I regrouped and ended up redeveloping that same site with a simpler build form that I knew the city officials would like. I stopped fighting and started listening. I gave them what they wanted and salvaged the relationship.

And in time I was given formal approvals to build eighteen townhomes on the site.

I'd assembled that particular plot of four detached homes for under $1 million, and when the appraisal for the land came in for our eighteen townhome lots, the value of the land alone shot up to $2.5 million. All by remaining laser focused on changing the use of the land and being conciliatory with the powers that be. In addition to the lift in the land, there were profits in the build out, while also creating cash flow in management fees, commissions, sub contractors contracts, etc.

In time I'd continue to leverage this same change-of-use template in a plethora of other projects in and around greater Toronto. Each acquisition was the direct result of building a strong relationship with sellers.

I was methodical, as you should be, in developing strategic short- and long-term business plans. I remained patient in looking for corner lots and assembling adjoining parcels around them. I listened carefully, throughout the whole process, to what various city planners expected of me. And, as a result, I became something of a community specialist in this particular pocket of Richmond Hill. A classic example of "onward and upward."

So here's some advice, distilled down to two simple bullet points: when working on change-of-use projects, you should (a) think and speak like an honest politician and (b) spend enough money to assemble the right group of consultants and experts.

Remember the old maxim: everyone is in favor of development and improvement unless it happens to be in their own backyard. Don't expect, even if your change-of-use plans make perfect sense, that you will get an approval without a fight.

I advise all budding real estate professionals who want to create real wealth to study civic plans and local policies. In the case of Toronto, as with most municipalities, the city's "official plan" is the document you should commit to memory. The arguments that you make before any municipal or local board must align with the key words and philosophies contained within that document.

Ask yourself all the necessary questions ahead of time. Does your project comply with current zoning restrictions or macro policies, such as the official plan or the provincial or state policy statements? Is it compatible with the character of the existing neighborhood? Does it support public transit? Have all your architectural and urban design responsibilities been fully accounted for and been properly budgeted for? Does it make sense in terms of established urban planning guidelines and philosophies?

By all means, be dogged in the pursuit of your vision, but don't be so bold as to try and ram your plan through the approval process without respecting municipal planners and city officials. It's better to be conciliatory and court municipal planners, city politicians, and local residents. While you can't always overcome political pressures, obtaining a positive planning report is essential in any project that might produce dissenting viewpoints.

In most cases hiring the best consultants that money can buy will be capital well spent. When I work on major projects, I hire a diverse array of partners. I often hire development consultants. Planners. Traffic and lighting consultants. Engineers. Landscape architects. Environmental experts. And of course a team of skilled and battle-tested municipal lawyers.

You should always allocate the necessary funds to complete first-rate studies and analyses, wherever and whenever they're needed.

Also make it a priority to ensure all of your consultants are involved from the start of the process so you don't run into problems with city planners and politicians late in the game.

That being said, as a developer, you still have to go with your gut and follow your instincts. You can't blindly follow people's advice, as you're ultimately the one responsible for making the final call.

Which is why I'd like to close with one more change-of-use story from my past, which I think is instructive in its own unique way. Beginning in 1997 I began purchasing a series of parcels in the Richmond Hills neighborhood: two along Church Street (115 and 119 Church Street) and two more along Major Mackenzie Drive (64 and 72 Major Mackenzie Drive).

Once again these parcels were located in an area that was being shown very little love or attention from other developers. There were a few rundown houses perched on the land, which weren't much to look at. But I kept accumulating anyway.

Unfortunately, I drew the ire of a neighbor who was hell-bent on halting any development near his property. Things got very con-tentious—to the point where he called a local newspaper and told a reporter that I was treating my tenants like a slumlord and fostering unsafe living conditions.

It was, of course, a complete lie. So when the reporter called me to comment, I conferenced him in with my tenants so that he could ask them if any of my neighbor's accusations were true. They said, "We have no complaints. We're happy to live here, and we are being treated perfectly well." Case closed. The reporter actually published the exact transcription of our conversation in his piece, completely vindicating me.

In regard to the project itself, I'd already spent a great deal of time studying the official plan for Richmond Hill, so I hired a law firm to develop a sophisticated proposal to build an eight-story building on the site. I had put a strong law firm and consulting team together to advocate for my application.

As I've previously mentioned, the OMB acted as a final arbiter for those hoping to appeal a decision. The board's job was to listen carefully to developers and consultants and weigh the merits of the application.

As you might expect, local municipalities did not want applications to go to the tribunal, because that would erode some of their say over the final decision. I've found that top-notch law firms and consulting teams can often create enough leverage to come to an amicable agreement that is beneficial for both the municipality in question and the developer.

Whenever I was asked to meet with planning officials, I made sure to field all their questions in person. I didn't send someone else. I accepted the responsibility of being the public face of my own project.

Once my team opened the door for a potential compromise, I removed them from the process. And I stepped back in to take the lead. I did so because, given my previous experiences, I'd built strong relationships with people in the planning department as well as local neighbors and politicians.

I knew I could be humble and noncombative in a way that most lawyers could not.

My formula for success: empathy in; profits out.

Whenever I was asked to meet with planning officials, I made sure to field all their questions in person. I didn't send someone else. I accepted the responsibility of being the public face of my own project.

In time I successfully negotiated a reduction in the project's height from eight stories to six stories, while also obtaining a positive planning report that was forwarded on to council. Not long after, the project was approved at the municipal level.

Ultimately, it was the various relationships I'd cultivated that won the day. I was able to get a six-story residential building approved along with two semidetached homes and two detached homes, all on the parcel. It was a different kind of change-of-use project—transitioning from single-family homes to an intensified built-form residential structure—but it was a profitable change of use nonetheless.

In the end I wound up selling that parcel for over $6 million, long before the building was ever erected. But the most enduring lesson of this episode, I think, lies in what happened between my disgruntled neighbor and me.

Once my six-story development was approved, I received word that my neighbor wanted to sell his property. Even though we had ostensibly gone to war with each other, my thoughts immediately snapped back to my OMB experience and my squabble with the commissioner. I'd patched things up by forgiving and forgetting, which has always served me well in the long run.

So why not swallow my pride, I thought, and do the same once again? Why not help my old nemesis get the best price for his lot and close the loop on this unfortunate disagreement? My neighbor actually reached out to me, which was a bit shocking.

I recall him telling me, "Let's face it, Dean: you won."

But I didn't view it that way at all. It wasn't a win-or-lose proposition. I explained to him that I sincerely believed that my development would benefit him as well.

As we got to talking, I think he realized I was being heartfelt and that I genuinely wanted to help him out. So we shook on a new deal, this time without anger and recriminations but rather with mutual respect and understanding for our respective positions.

I assumed that the investors who bought my parcel would be interested in his as well. And sure enough my wife wound up brokering the sale of my neighbor's lot for a very good price with the same people who bought my land. My wife is a very humble and empathetic person, two qualities that I've learned go a very long way toward ensuring every change-of-use project, whether large or small, starts well and ends even better. Hopefully, after reading about some of my change-of-use projects, you can see the wisdom of that sentiment as well.

CHAPTER 6

THE ONASSIS EFFECT:
THE ART OF SALESMANSHIP AND
THE CRAFT OF CREATIVE FINANCING

I wonder how many young real estate agents have ever heard the name Aristotle Onassis, let alone know much about the legendary shipping magnate's business philosophies.

These days Onassis is probably best remembered for swooping in, after the tragic assassination of John F. Kennedy, and parlaying a friendship with JFK's wife, Jackie, into a marriage proposal.

In the 1960s Aristotle's courtship of Jackie attracted as much ink from the tabloids as Lady Diana's life would generate three decades later. But I'm not interested one iota in the man's love life.

What fascinates me—and what may prove very instructive to you—is the fearlessness Onassis showed in taking bold risks and leveraging smart financing to amass one of the largest armadas of seaborne transports the world has ever seen.

Note that all-important key word "financing"? Ever notice how rare it is for the multilevel marketers in our profession to devote more than a passing mention of that topic during their speeches?

Curious as to why that's the case? Because the art of helping buyers overcome financial hurdles doesn't translate very well into talking points and trite sound bites.

Creative financing demands an entrepreneurial mindset and actual real-world business experience, two things that are often sorely lacking in our industry.

My pitch to you? Think like an entrepreneur, not a spin doctor. Raising capital, if I may be so blunt, is more than half the battle, whether you're representing buyers or developing a piece of land for yourself.

And to raise capital, you have to be willing to push the envelope in terms of how you structure deals, and then make some gutsy moves to close them.

Which brings us, full circle, back to Aristotle Onassis.

I'm by no means an Onassis biographer, but I became interested in his business philosophies during the 1990s, while I was enrolled in an entrepreneurship class at Ryerson University in Toronto.

At the time, I was busy making a turn away from selling eco-friendly cleaning products. While in my twenties, I'd launched and nurtured my own company, Principally Green, yet found myself magnetically drawn to a potential career in real estate.

I'd inherited my sales abilities from my father. He's always looked at the world the way a professional poker player views a high-stakes card game. He's a "no-bet-is-too-big" kind of guy. Just like I am.

I remember, as a teenager, being crowned the top-selling chocolate salesman at my school. Bringing home the annual $500 grand prize was always gratifying, but selling chocolates didn't feel like work to me. I genuinely enjoyed the challenge of going door to door and talking to perfect strangers about the superior taste and quality of my candy.

I sold those chocolate-covered almonds to pretty much everyone and anyone in my orbit. Family. Friends. Neighbors. Other kids.

After all, who doesn't like an occasional nibble of chocolate every now and again?

Sales came naturally to me, so much so that I remember my principal once standing before everyone in my school and saying, "Listen, I'm not asking all of you to be like Dean Artenosi and sell twenty boxes of chocolate a day, but can you, at least, try to sell a few boxes this year?"

I learned, very early in life, that profits are best reinvested, rather than being squandered or deposited into a low-interest savings account.

When I was sixteen, for instance, I received an injury settlement after being struck by a car. Instead of wasting the money, I invested every last dime into starting what turned out to be a rather successful carpet-cleaning business.

Later, I joined Vector and Cutco, where some really smart people helped me hone my craft and develop my ability to close deals. As I've noted before, guys like Adam Ginsberg and Joe Gruskin were extraordinary mentors who reinforced the importance of hard work and passion. They lived and embodied the "onward and upward" mindset that is at the heart of this book.

Thanks to their guidance and my dogged commitment to make the most out of my time there, I became, virtually overnight, the top-ranked salesman of Cutco kitchen knives in all of Canada.

In the years that followed, I continued to exhibit the kinds of traits and idiosyncrasies most people associate with entrepreneurs. I cranked out ideas the way Snickers churns out chocolate bars. I hustled—morning, noon, and night—365 days a year and showed an eagerness to assume risks that would've scared away 99 percent of the general population.

But I don't think I actualized my true potential as a salesman or entrepreneur until I joined the real estate world and realized just how vital risk-taking and creative financing are in generating wealth in any business.

Let me be clear: my aim is not to encourage you to take on the same amount of risk that I shouldered over the course of my career. I understand that everyone's appetite for risk is unique. But I do want to stress how highly correlated risk tolerance is to long-term success and how important an entrepreneurial mindset is in building a self-sustaining career in real estate, whether you're an agent or developer.

It comes down to this: it's not the size of the risk you take, especially early in your career, that matters so much as your openness to seize opportunities wherever they may materialize.

Take Aristotle Onassis, for example. You'd be hard pressed to find a historian who wouldn't credit Onassis with being one of the boldest and most fearless risk-takers of the twentieth century.

Here was a man who launched a massively successful cigarette company while he was still in his twenties. In fact, he built it purely on a hunch—namely that an uptick in smoking by stars and starlets on the silver screen would encourage moviegoers to rush out and mimic their habits at home.

The tobacco business made young Aristotle a millionaire practically overnight. But when he recognized that transporting tobacco could turn a larger profit than selling it, Onassis immediately set a new goal for himself: he'd invest the bulk of his profits into acquiring the largest private shipping fleet possible during the Great Depression.

The inherent risks in starting a new business during such uncertain times didn't dissuade him one bit. If anything, he saw the downturn as a golden opportunity because sea captains the world over seemed willing to sell their ships for pennies on the dollar.

It was likely the size and scope of Onassis's ambitions—not to mention his unmatched fearlessness—that attracted the attention of the US government, which viewed him as one of the few industrial-ists capable of shipping a steady supply of oil and military supplies to Allied forces stationed overseas during World War II.

Which brings me to one of my favorite Aristotle Onassis stories. To this day I can't verify if the story my professor told us was actually true, but the anecdote, as it was communicated to me, goes something like this:

When Aristotle Onassis entered into negotiations with the US government for shipping contracts, he didn't own enough ships to transport the specific number of supplies outlined in the contract.

He employed what I'd call, with all due respect, a classic "fake-it-till-you-make-it" strategy.

Once Onassis signed that contract with the US government, he worked backward from his newfound position of strength. With that piece of paper in hand, he knew that he could stroll into any banker's office, slide that document across the desk, and tell any loan officer in the land, "I have the full faith and credit of the United States govern-ment behind me. Give me some money, please."

What bank could refuse his request, knowing that Uncle Sam was in his corner?

And sure enough Onassis's little gambit proved extraordinarily successful. Bankers *did* line up to loan him all the capital that he needed. He then used those funds to buy more ships and fulfilled his obligations to the United States.

Like any good real estate investor, Onassis brokered a deal that made him money in the immediate term as well as the long term, as profits, year after year, compounded into astronomical sums of money.

Which is the *exact* same goal you should set for yourself in the real estate game.

As I listened to my professor's lectures on Onassis, I remember sitting up arrow straight in my wobbly chair and thinking to myself, "That's it. That's the *secret* knowledge."

It hit me like a lightning bolt sent straight from Mount Olympus itself. Entrepreneurs don't negotiate based on what they can do in the present moment. Ultimately, their goal is to make deals based on what they'll be able to achieve once a deal is done.

That was exactly the kind of thinking, I whispered to myself, that I needed to apply to my new career in real estate.

And I hope you'll follow his lead in your career too.

Remember: your job, at the end of the day, is to help your clients solve problems. As such, you don't want to limit yourself by thinking too chronologically.

It doesn't matter if your dream seems slightly unattainable in the early going. Formulate a plan. Push yourself and your clients to take some risks. And you'll be shocked at how often you can transform lofty dreams into profitable realities.

Selling Is a Process: Start with the Dream

As it turns out, Aristotle Onassis's sales strategies weren't very different from my own.

I think both Mr. Onassis and I would agree on the following maxim: it doesn't matter what you're selling—kitchen knives or cars or real estate—you need to sell a product in stages, rather than in one high-pressure push. I learned this invaluable truth while selling Cutco knives.

A good set of '90s-era Cutco knives wasn't exactly cheap, so I never went out of my way to talk prices until very late in a conversation. Defining *why* a product (or new home) is needed comes first; outlining *how* that purchase can be achieved comes later.

Your first goal, especially in real estate, is to stick your foot into the proverbial doorjamb and convince people it's in their best interests to invite you into their living room. Because once you're able to observe where a client is currently living, you can paint a tantalizing picture of where they *could* be living instead.

> **It doesn't matter what you're selling— kitchen knives or cars or real estate— you need to sell a product in stages, rather than in one high-pressure push.**

Let's say you're speaking to a potential client with a growing family who is clearly running out of room in their current place. Or young newlyweds basking in the glow of their recent nuptials. Or an elderly couple looking to downsize.

If you understand their unique situation—their individual needs—you can always use those facts to your advantage.

Encourage them to tell you what they *don't* currently love about their home, so that they begin rattling off all the things they hope to have in their next home. Maybe it's a finished basement. A bigger yard. Or a two-car garage so they aren't forced to park on the street.

Good salesmanship, like creative financing, is all about comparing a future reality to an existing one. My advice: get a lay of the land. Understand why your clients want to make a move. And then immediately pack them up into a car and get them out on the road to start seeing properties.

You can't dawdle. You can't sit back and wait for a potential client to request a site visit. You have to take them out as quickly as you can, so that they begin to view you, as their agent, as an indispensable facilitator of their dreams.

While you're driving them around to see various properties, start conducting credit checks, compile income statements, and begin mapping out what types of financing options might be available to them. Your initial aim is to get a sense of just how much money your clients can spend and then provide them workarounds to raise the amount of money they actually need to make the move.

The key, as noted in the aforementioned Aristotle Onassis story, is to keep your client focused on the future. Keep them excited and dreaming about the prospect of moving into a new home that suits their current needs.

You want to maintain forward momentum, which will invariably motivate people to accept the risks required to obtain sufficient financing.

A mentor of mine once told me that both buyers' agents and real estate developers have a responsibility to stick as close to the truth as possible. And I agree wholeheartedly with that sentiment. But the real truth of the matter is that most people can afford to move into nicer homes if they're willing to take on additional risk to do so. Your clients will buy on emotion and the dream of homeownership, and they will justify with the logic of how they can finance the purchase and why it is a smart decision and worth all the risk.

Here are some tips and strategies that can help your clients achieve just that laudable goal.

Strategy 1: Encourage First-Time Homeowners to Use Their Rental Deposits

When in doubt, keep things simple. In Ontario every renter must provide their landlord with their first and last month's rent deposit to secure a premises for lease. As such, there should be two months that the tenant will not have to make a monthly rental payment when they vacate that premises.

It's very common for first-time home buyers to completely forget about these funds, even though they can be instrumental in cobbling together a down payment or covering closing costs.

Given today's increasingly steep rental costs, those deposits can really add up. In most cases people will be able to bank two months of rent totaling $5,000 to $10,000 or more. All you need to do, as their agent, is convince your clients *not* to squander that money the minute it comes boomeranging back to them.

How do you do that? By reminding them of all the benefits they're going to experience in the future after they move into their new home.

So don't let long stretches of time pass without calling your clients. Keep in contact with them. Remind them what's on the other side of the rainbow and how a short-term sacrifice can yield a plethora of long-term benefits down the road. In some sense you have to be a psychologist as much as a real estate agent.

It also never hurts to remind first-time home buyers that their first mortgage payment isn't due until thirty days after closing. Mortgages always run thirty days behind, whereas rent is prepaid. Psychologically, it helps some home buyers to know that they have a little extra cushion at their disposal after they move into their new home.

Think Onassis, think entrepreneurial, think ultimate service.

Strategy 2: Encourage Your Clients to Ask Friends and Family for Help

It's amazing how quickly some real estate agents give up when a client tells them that they don't know *anyone*—friend, family member, coworker—who is willing to gift or loan them money to help pay for a down payment.

My advice? Keep probing. Remind your clients that there's nothing wrong with asking for a little help. Early in my career, I certainly asked for help. Although I didn't particularly *want* to do it, I did wind up asking my parents for $5,000 to help me enroll in a real estate class, and they obliged.

I recount this story to my clients all the time. You should do the same. Try telling them a story from your own past that will encourage them to reach out to loved ones to help cover their loan.

I don't think it's wrong—in fact, I think it's honest—to remind people that friends and family are the people we always rely on in times of need.

In most cases there's usually someone who would be willing to help out, provided, of course, your client musters up the courage to ask.

Try posing this simple question to your clients to help nudge them along: *If someone in your family desperately needed financial help and you were holding on to a little extra money, would you help them out?*

In most cases a client will nod their head and say, "Sure."

If that's the case, ask them why the reverse would be any different. In most cases loans evolve into a kind of quid pro quo over time. You were here for me when I needed you, so I'll return the favor when you need my help in the future.

A quick story to prove this point: One of my agents once approached me and said that she was working with a lovely client— let's call her Mary—who'd fallen deeply and madly in love with a single-family home just outside of Toronto. Only the mortgage officer who was analyzing her earnings refused to offer her a loan.

Mary had a respectable salary, but due to the COVID-19 lockdowns, she'd been forced to take on hourly gigs instead of full-time work. And, as you probably know, when a potential borrower works hourly, most banks will ask to see two years of average hourly earnings.

Given that COVID-19 had pretty much shut down the world, Mary didn't have a particularly impressive two-year average. Since the offer she'd made was conditional on financing, she worried that the prospect of buying her dream home was quickly slipping through her fingers.

The easiest solution? Find a cosigner.

But Mary told my agent there was no way anyone, friend or family, would agree to be a cosigner. Figuring that his client had hit a dead end, my agent simply left it at that.

Only I suggested that we push Mary a little harder. I called her up and asked a few follow-up questions:

Were her parents still alive? No.

Aunts and uncles? No.

Okay, how about siblings? Mary paused. As it turned out, she did have a younger sister, but she didn't dare ask her for help because she was just starting her career.

I pressed a little more. What kind of work did her sister do? Turned out Mary's sister had a really good job, especially for her age.

If Mary's sister agreed to be a cosigner, it would only take Mary two years to assume back control over the mortgage (as two years of steady work would bump her average back up high enough to fulfill the bank's requirement). I also asked Mary if her sister needed help in the future to get into her own home, would she return the favor? Mary said, "Of course I would."

Furthermore, we could put her sister down as a 1 percent owner, thereby protecting her ownership stake. A separate indemnity agreement could be structured with her sister, guaranteeing that Mary would indemnify her sister from all liabilities.

As far as I was concerned, this was a no-brainer. Our client had to call her sister ASAP.

And sure enough, after a little hemming and hawing, Mary did ring her sister, who agreed to the deal—knowing full well that when she needed help in the future, her kindness would be paid back in kind.

Faster than you could say, "family ties," the loan was approved, allowing Mary to move into the starter home of her dreams. Timing is everything. Had I asked Mary to make that call earlier, there's a good chance she would have rebuffed us.

In the end she overcame her fears because the prospect of moving into her new home outweighed the stress of making the call. We showed her a better future, while reminding her, ever so gently, of what she needed to do to achieve it. And she did just that. She made it happen with nothing more than a single phone call.

Getting preapprovals is a good idea; however, as mentioned already there is a sales process, and clients want to be sold in stages. In this case we had to get the client in the conditional time period of an accepted offer for her to drum up the courage and overcome her pride and ask her family for help. At this stage the opportunity of homeownership is at the client's fingertips, so if you can get a client to this stage, they will find a way to make it happen. You are definitely taking a chance and risk to take a client out looking at homes knowing the financing requires hurdles to overcome.

Think Onassis, think entrepreneurial, think ultimate service.

Strategy 3: Leverage the RRSP and Mutual Fund Opportunities

As I previously mentioned, I created the first no-money-down buyer programs in Canada during the mid-1990s.

I began by running a series of newspaper ads touting my no-money-down plans. And to be honest, I was shocked by how many phone calls came flooding in.

Old and young, married and single—virtually everyone told me that they didn't want to be renters anymore; only they had no clue how to amass enough money for a proper down payment.

It should be noted that, unlike today, you could buy a respectable single-family home or condo in the Toronto area for $180,000 to $200,000. I also knew that the Canada Mortgage and Housing Corporation (CMHC) would support anyone who could scrounge up a 5 percent down payment.

My simple goal? Devise some creative ways to help all these potential buyers come up with $10,000.

Thanks to my eco-friendly cleaning product company, I'd developed some strong relationships with bank lenders, which gave me an advantage over some of my real estate peers.

The problem, of course, was that my contacts weren't going to lend $10,000 to people who had zero collateral. One afternoon, after researching Canada's Registered Retirement Savings Program (RRSP), I formulated an outside-the-box plan.

Fact No. 1: The Canadian government actively encouraged people to buy into RRSPs, as they were safe, government-backed retirement vehicles.

Fact No. 2: If Canadians withdrew money out of their RRSPs for everyday expenses, those withdrawals would be taxed at a rate of 20 or 30 percent.

Fact No. 3: The RRSP was offering a first-time home buyer program, which allowed people to withdraw RRSP funds without paying any taxes, provided they paid back their withdrawal within fifteen years.

Fact No. 4: Unfortunately, no one who opened a new RRSP could directly use the funds as a down payment unless they held it for a full ninety days.

Fact No. 5: Anyone who contributed to their RRSP was eligible to claim a 30 percent rebate on those contributions when they filed their taxes that same year.

Round and round these facts went swimming in my mind, until it hit me.

What if I encouraged my clients to take out a $20,000 loan from one of my bank contacts to open up their own RRSP? After all, RRSP loans were easily approved by most banks.

After they put the money in the RRSP and waited ninety days, my clients could visit a different lender and ask for a mortgage application. The loan officer would see that they were holding a viable $20,000 asset and approve a mortgage for them.

Come tax time my clients could reap the benefits of having opened their RRSP by accepting their government-mandated rebate. They could then use those extra funds to start paying off their original loan or cover other expenses.

In Canada a bank cannot use an RRSP as security for a loan. It can for a mutual fund or an investment. The loans we are talking about are not large sums of money. Therefore, what I would do is just withdraw the RRSP under the first home buyers' program, and in many cases clients did not have to pay back the loan they took out to buy the RRSP. Sometimes, the bank will make you sign an irrevocable direction, which is another way for the bank to ensure you pay back the loan it gave you if you withdraw the RRSP before the loan is paid back.

> **One thing you can always rely on is the bank's appetite for business.**

One thing you can always rely on is the bank's appetite for business.

Another creative way to utilize the RRSP is to have the client take out a loan secured against personal assets, such as vehicles. They could then utilize these funds to buy an investment such as a mutual fund or an RRSP. This will free up the RRSP or investment, which allows your client to withdraw the funds for the down payment on the home.

It's a process that worked wonders for my clients and continues to work for home buyers to this very day.

Think Onassis, think entrepreneurial, think ultimate service.

Strategy 4: Make Your Client a Subcontractor

There's a program called the purchase plus improvement program offered through the mortgage insurers, which allows you to obtain a mortgage and add the construction cost onto the mortgage as one package with a 5 percent down payment product. This concept can be done with conventional financing as well, so it's not a new concept.

You're unlikely to secure a mortgage if you act as your own contractor. The banks will not permit this, as you are not at arm's length. You can, however, have your client act as a subcontractor of the general contractor when the work is being completed, which is a private matter between the homeowner and the general contractor. I highly recommend this if you're a buyer's agent who's working with a trusted general contractor. This is called sweat equity.

I relied on the program a great deal in the past. Here's how I did it: because I owned my own construction company, I could hire new homeowners who were capable of doing work on their own homes to help them earn back part of their renovation costs.

The work could be as simple as painting walls, or perhaps your client is a skilled trades person or can do something as labor intensive as demolition and cleanup. Depending on the skill level of your client, they can choose accordingly.

In our case I simply computed how much money it would cost us to perform the aforementioned work, and then I paid the homeowner for performing this task. These deals proved to be a win-win for new homeowners then and continue to aid renters who need a little extra cash to buy a new home today. It is very labor intensive, and there are risks associated with this concept, such as avoiding construction liens, customer and contractor disputes, or financing the construction costs until completion.

Think Onassis, think entrepreneurial, think ultimate service.

Strategy 5: Explore Short-Term High-Interest Loans

When you run into a real brick wall, you can always encourage a client to explore taking out high-interest loans, which require borrowers to put up worthwhile assets as collateral.

Some of these lending agencies will accept an old car as an asset, whereas some triple-A banks will not. Buyers must ensure they're dealing with reputable lenders and must do everything in their power to pay off their loans as soon as possible, because the interest rates on these products can be exorbitant.

A quick caveat: once a bank approves the mortgage and your client becomes a homeowner, their bank will look at them completely differently. Their bank will likely want *all* the lender's business: Visa, MasterCard, lines of credit, etc. Fortunately, your client can ask their mortgage lender to take over the high-interest loans after they've moved in, provided they've made several monthly payments.

Short-term high-interest loans are not an easy fix, but should your client need a quick $10,000 that they can pay back quickly, it's certainly something worth looking into.

Think Onassis, think entrepreneurial, think ultimate service.

Just as Onassis took his entrepreneurial creative financing skill from his earlier beginnings in the tobacco industry to bigger and higher levels of success, so too can you—which leads us to our next chapter.

CHAPTER 7

TAKING THE NEXT STEP:
LEVERAGING RISK AS A
REAL ESTATE DEVELOPER

All these aforementioned strategies I've outlined in the book thus far have two things in common: they require an openness to risk-taking and a willingness to think like an entrepreneur.

It wasn't until I completed my entrepreneurship class at Ryerson that I realized how few people working in real estate have the ability to look at the world through an entrepreneurial lens. So, if you put in the time required to develop those skills, you'll leapfrog over 90 percent of your peers.

Why, you might be wondering, are there so few entrepreneurs in our space?

Because young real estate agents are taught, very early in their careers, to focus all their effort on honing their marketing skills rather than learning how to work the numbers.

Some might argue that an entrepreneurial mindset can't be taught, that you're either born with it or you're not. That risk-taking is an inherited trait, not unlike blue eyes or curly hair.

While there may be a filament of truth to that idea, I maintain that it's entirely possible, given proper encouragement, to bolster your risk tolerance and financial acumen.

As I've previously noted, I believe the primary goal of real estate agents and brokers is to provide the best service possible to your clients. At the end of the day, we're tasked with trying to devise practical solutions to extremely knotty problems.

My advice: seek out a financial niche for yourself. And pursue that niche with dogged determination. Odds be damned.

For me it was helping renters become first-time homeowners. And then using my newfound knowledge to build increasingly complex—and profitable—development projects.

To date I have helped over 4,500 families purchase homes they otherwise wouldn't have been able to afford. I helped many of them buy homes with very little down and helped others use nothing more than their rent deposits. I'm very proud of that legacy, but I'm equally proud of what I did with the money I earned from helping them.

So, slip back in time with me to the early 2000s, when I decided to start putting these tools to work for my own development business.

I'd been dreaming of spearheading larger projects for years, but my initial meetings with loan officers made me feel as if that dream still lay slightly beyond my reach.

On paper I certainly wasn't the greatest candidate to secure major loans. At the time I didn't have a bankable track record of developing anything larger than a few single-family homes. I had zero management experience. And I had saved what could only be described as a modest amount of cash.

Nevertheless, I was committed, à la Aristotle Onassis, to faking my *bona fides* until I could earn them for myself.

My goal was to build a twenty-four-stack townhouse development on a parcel of land located at 125 Hall Street. When my construction partner and I visited a local loan agent, he sat us down and explained, in a somber tone, the rules of the game.

He informed us that the only way anyone would ever consider— he put extra stress on the word *consider*—loaning us money for a project of this size was if we met three strict requirements.

No. 1: We would be required to presell roughly 70 percent of our townhome units before the bank released our first construction draw.

No. 2: As developers, we would have to invest enough money in the project—whether that was equity in land, funding project costs, or both—to cover key project milestones as well as potential overruns.

And No. 3: We would need to prove to the bank that we had amassed sufficient experience working on a project of this size and scale.

Suffice to say my partner and I would not be able to fulfill any of these prerequisites, especially the last. We'd never taken a project of this size on before, so how could we show a track record of success?

When our loan approval was rejected, I initially grew very despondent. How in the world, I wondered, does a successful real estate agent transition into becoming a developer if no one is willing to lend them enough money to prove they could succeed?

Luckily, I stuck with it. And in time a lucky break came our way.

I managed to arrange a meeting with Bob Lynch, who worked for Murray & Company, a sophisticated brokerage house that's been funding construction projects and developers since the early 1900s.

Suffice to say Bob and I hit it off right away, and he made it clear to me that he believed in my vision for the Hall Street project as well as my sales abilities.

Ultimately, Bob was the reason—along with a key financing commitment from Laurentian Bank—that I was able to set my Hall Street project in motion.

Since there were two residential homes located on the site, I'd acquired the land by securing two residential mortgages. And since I was partnering with my uncle, Anthony Fusco, and a fellow construction professional named Sam Dipasquale, to build the townhomes, I was working with people I could trust.

The problem, of course, was that I'd have to spearhead all our marketing efforts and secure presale agreements for our townhomes—all while communicating with our lenders, gaining construction approvals, overseeing presales construction draws, and handling monthly audits from our construction lender.

The lesson? You'll never feel ready to take the leap from being a real estate agent to a developer. *You just have to do it.* As Onassis has taught us, just stay focused on your end goals and move backward from there.

> **You'll never feel ready to take the leap from being a real estate agent to a developer. *You just have to do it.***

It will feel, at times, like you've descended into the fifth circle of hell. Your time will never feel like it's your own. Nevertheless, you can't give in to those fears.

Remember: entrepreneurs and real estate developers must be willing to take risks that 95 percent of the general public would run away from.

As we attempted to get our Hall Street development up and running, there were plenty of naysayers who doubted we would succeed. After all, we'd drawn up a unique structure, which included an underground parking garage that was years ahead of its time. But in the end, we persevered. We built our $8 million townhouse development on Hall Street, which we called the Manor of Mill Pond.

And lo and behold, as soon as we finished, we started attracting the attention of new investors.

My advice: after completing your first project, strike while the iron is still hot.

Don't rest on your laurels. Harness all that goodwill and all that newfound attention you've amassed to immediately jump into your next project, because positive momentum is a rare, rare thing. As I've said time and again, there's only one direction to fly: onward and upward.

In our case I partnered with an investor who had helped back me when I was putting together my Georgian Bay deal.

I was elated, of course, but I also realized that we didn't have nearly enough capital to fund the project I was envisioning, as I wanted to transition from building townhomes to erecting midsize condominiums and eventually high-rise condominiums.

I outlined a plan to build a thirty-three-unit condo building on Hunt Avenue, which we dubbed the Rosehill Suites project. In addition we also acquired a different parcel at 2464 Weston Road, where we hoped to build a second condo development called Riverside Suites.

Some people will warn you against getting too ambitious as a young developer. But is it too realpolitik of me to confess that I believe that you often have to do just that? Truth is, finding yourself a little over your skis is the only way to make a real leap forward in your real estate career.

If you're not prepared to balance the weight of the world on your shoulders and literally live on the razor's edge, you're simply not ready to be a developer.

In the case of Rosehill and Riverside Suites, I knew we didn't have enough capital to build these buildings, nor enough experience to secure funding from a big bank, so we struck a deal with a private investor.

Since we desperately wanted to build these condos, we agreed to a contract that was dramatically one-sided in our investor's favor.

The deal, as signed, came down to this: our investor would put up all the money, while my partners and I would provide a personal guarantee on that loan, in addition to all the construction financing.

Our investor would put up all the money via a secured mortgage on the land. He also obtained personal guarantees from us, meaning that we were responsible for covering all the interest that accrued on that mortgage. Despite the enormous risk we were taking on, he'd still own 50 percent of the project through a separate corporation that he owned.

You can probably see where this is going, can't you?

I was tasked with acting as a kind of mediator between our investor and my construction partners. But as the project progressed, a fracture in their relationship began to create serious problems. Although I did my best to try to mend that fissure, I could tell that things were going to continue to go south really quickly.

What I'm about to describe is a little technical, but stay with me here, as it's important for new developers to understand the complexities of these deals: we had arranged for an interest reserve to carry the loan and to fund costs built into the mortgage. Alas, these funds quickly ran out. As a result my investor convinced us that it would be wise to refinance his loan and raise more capital to cover all these new costs.

We agreed, but meanwhile, our investor convinced his solicitors to find another investor who might be interested in refinancing our mortgage. Even though our original investor received all his money plus interest, we would still have to personally guarantee the new loan. Once we paid our original investor all the money he was due, he informed us that he'd be exiting the project.

I can remember his exact words to me: "Sometimes no matter how much money is to be made, it's just not worth it."

Looking back I believe his entire strategy was premeditated. I don't think he had any intention of seeing this project through to completion after he got his money back plus interest. As a result my partners and I were now left holding the bag. We were responsible for coming up with the full $3.5 million plus interest.

So, be forewarned: crises of this magnitude can and often do occur when you agree to a one-sided deal. So don't let anyone tell you that real estate isn't a speculative business, because it is.

Looking back I realize that we signed a deal that was, in my opinion, weighed too much in his favor. I know the old maxim that says, "He who holds the money holds the gold" is true. But one-sided deals don't usually end up working in the end.

In his mind he was putting up all the money. But the dispute between both parties (my management partners and my investor) ramped up. And in the end, I just found it too difficult to bridge the gap. I think I understand what he meant with his exact words. In the end it just wasn't worth it for either party.

Our original investor had negotiated interest *plus* a 50 percent equity position. In retrospect I realize that was simply too much to ask of us. But at the time, I was willing to do anything to finish the project. I wanted it *that* badly.

I subscribe to the philosophy that says, *If you worry too much about what the other guy is going to make on a deal, you'll never make anything yourself.*

The best deals, in my opinion, are rooted in that old Three Musketeer mantra: what's best for one party should be best for all parties involved.

Suffice to say you have to start somewhere, and we paid the price for that bumpy start. While my investor elected not to proceed with the project, he certainly didnt' hold a gun to our heads on the agreement, and he also left us with an opportunity. In the end I know he genuinely wanted us to succeed. This individual was someone that I respected tremendously and learned a great deal from and hold in the highest regards still to this day.

> **If you worry too much about what the other guy is going to make on a deal, you'll never make anything yourself.**

It helped, of course, that we'd bought quality parcels at a good price. And I knew in my heart of hearts that the final profits, should we survive this current chaos, would be worth all the stress.

So, I reached out to my original investor's lawyer and explained that it was in everyone's best interests for my partners and me to finish the job. He had assumed that we'd simply liquidate the property—fire sale the whole thing—lick our wounds and call it a day.

But I was having none of that. I desperately wanted to complete the project. So I did my best to convince my investor's lawyer that it was in everyone's best interests that we finish what we set out to do.

After all, if we were to complete the projects successfully, this would benefit his client, as we'd be able to cover his initial investment plus interest. His lawyer agreed, and he helped us to get the project off the ground and ultimately complete it.

Needless to say my partners and I were still staring down the barrel of bankruptcy.

My first goal? Secure financing for the Rosehill Suites project. This time the lender in question was Peoples Trust, but the key player was a loan officer by the name of Jim Dysart.

Dysart agreed to meet with me because he'd gone to school with my father, but when I sat down with him—along with Bob Lynch, my mortgage broker, who remained by my side—my plan for the project was sound enough that he agreed to help me.

To complete this new deal, we had to negotiate a separate deal with a mezzanine lender who'd be willing to take second position on a first mortgage construction loan of roughly $7 million.

At the time, mezzanine lenders were charging upward of 18 percent, which proved to be an expensive add-on, yet the deal remained better than us giving up 50 percent of our profits by hooking up with another equity partner. We closed our mezzanine deal so we could make a partial pay down to our new investor.

It was Creative Financing 101, from start to finish.

In regard to the project itself, we had another major issue to contend with. Although we'd already gained approval to build twenty-six units for our Rosehill Suites condominium, our ultimate goal was to add seven additional units to the building.

Fortunately, we'd included large terraces into the original building's design, which we hoped to convert into extra condos.

It was my job to convince *all* parties involved—construction lenders, our mezzanine lender, our new investor—that attaining this increase in density was, indeed, possible.

To win approval for these thirty-three units, I told the local planning commissioner that I'd build whatever she wanted on a separate project I was working on at Benson and Hall Streets. The council and the commissioner agreed to my proposal, allowing me to snatch victory (not to mention a thirty-three-unit condominium) from the certain jaws of bankruptcy.

But just as Aristotle Onassis used proceeds from his cigarette company to purchase his transportation fleet, I knew that completing our Rosehill Suites condo project was only half the battle. I'd need to press on and quickly switch over to our second project, the Riverside Suites condominium on Weston Road.

As any developer will tell you, going from our $8 million loan for the thirty-three-unit six-story Rosehill condo to $20 million in financing for our proposed ten-story 163-unit Riverside condo was a major jump, akin to being called up from an NHL affiliate to the actual NHL.

Fortunately, I had developed a strong enough relationship with Jim Dysart that he decided to support me once again. I impressed the hell out of him when I secured those seven additional units approved for Rosehill Suites, but the $20 million construction loan that I now needed for Riverside was too big for Jim and Peoples Trust to take on alone.

So, Jim brokered a joint venture to sew up the construction loan. In essence Peoples Trust would take $5 million of the deal, and the British Columbia Investment Management Corporation (BCI) pension fund would accept the remaining $12 million for the first mortgage on our construction loan. Our insurers took their lien in second position for the surety bond that we needed to post to Tarion, which is the governing body for builders, and of course our investor mortgage followed that in third position.

Peoples Trust acted as the administrator of the loan for both parties, Peoples Trust and the BCI pension fund for the first mortgage. The risks were as nerve-racking and stomach churning as ever.

Our new investor's land mortgage would have to be postponed and slotted into a third position behind $20 million of mortgages. The Guarantee Company of North America was in second position, and of course Peoples Trust and BCI pension fund were in first position.

The new land mortgages were nonconstruction/developer lenders. They'd only allow this to happen if we provided them security outside of the deal for their mortgage. My partners and I did just that. We put up our *own* homes for collateral in order for this project to proceed.

This financing was complicated. It was a high-risk, high-stakes proposition. At any time throughout this process, the bank could've pulled the plug on us, and we'd lose everything.

Talk about risky! Try coming home to your wife and newborn twins every night, as I did, with all this hanging over your head. Looking back it was probably the most stressful period of my life, in what I must admit has been a stress-filled but oh-so-rewarding career in real estate.

Suffice to say there were innumerable factors and variables that had to lock perfectly into place for a complex financing deal like this to work, but in the end it did.

I'll go through a few of them. As I previously mentioned, one of the chief obstacles we faced involved the fact that our condo backed up against the Humber River.

The unforeseen problem? Half of the bank went and collapsed on us when we were getting approvals.

As a result we had to cleave off a section of the building and shrink the building's overall envelope, setting it back far enough so that it didn't adversely impact the river at all.

We also had to jump through multiple hoops that were thrown at us by the Toronto Regional Conservation Authority so that we could obtain a final site plan approval and all the necessary permits.

I remember the owner of my sales company at the time, Brad Lamb, who is now a major developer in Toronto, pulling me aside one day and telling me, "If you pull off this deal, Dean, you can pull off anything."

What got me through it? The exact same things that will get you through the project you're going to pursue once you close the back cover of this book: risk-taking. Grit. Creative financing. And an entrepreneurial "onward and upward" mindset.

Everything and anything that could go wrong in that deal did go wrong. We had to deal with trades and large contractors who would play the legal extortion game of billing us for extras. As you might know, if you are over budget on a project like this, the lender requires you to ante up and pay for overruns out of your own pocket.

And if a contractor places liens on your property, your lender will stop giving you funding until that lien is settled or bonded. Bonding a lien requires that you, as the developer, pay off said lien plus an extra 25 percent in court. The lender freezes until that's settled, even though the interest accrued on the loan does not.

We didn't have the capital to bond liens. Our forming contractor had a bad reputation for swallowing up trades and landowners by playing the legal extortion game. They were threatening to lien our site for an extra $300,000. I settled the matter by negotiating a condo unit valued for $300,000, promising to give them a condo unit after the project was completed.

Any time my construction partner found himself in a disagreement with a trade or contractor, the lender always looked to me to resolve it. It *always* fell back on me.

Truth is this particular deal included more financial pressures and involved a level of risk that most people probably wouldn't be able to sustain.

Want to know the secret to my success? It was all those years I'd spent solving problems for buyers. And all those years I'd spent trying to be creative and resourceful when it came to financing.

I'd learned to make thing happen so often, for so many different people, that I knew, in the end, I could make this deal work. Making money when you buy real estate and buying with very little down payment, if any, creating sweat equity—I was doing just this, only on a large scale.

It was creative financing on steroids! But I did what Aristotle Onassis would have done. I saw the solution and worked backward, step by step, to make it a reality.

In the end the building was finished, the joint venture was a success, and everybody walked away with a sizable profit.

Something tells me, with a little grit and an expanded appetite for risk, you can do the same. So that's *my* secret knowledge: help others build wealth through creative financing, and, the next thing you know, you'll be doing the same, with exponentially greater returns waiting for you at the end of it all.

CHAPTER 8

PASSION MEETS PURPOSE:
GOING BACK TO THE FUTURE WITH THE NEW URBANISM MOVEMENT

Not long ago I happened upon a story that asked an important question: "Why aren't young people buying homes anymore?"[7]

It was the kind of stat-heavy piece that I enjoy digging into because it refused to prescribe easy answers to what's undoubtedly a complex and multifaceted question.

I was simultaneously encouraged and saddened by what I read, as some of the piece's findings made me want to cheer, while others made me want to pull my hair out.

So where to start? Do you want the good news or the bad news first? The lemons or the lemonade?

Let's begin with the sweet stuff first, shall we? The dream of homeownership, by all indications, seems to be alive and well in North America, especially among millennials and Gen Zers.

---

7   Tom Huddleston Jr., "Millennials and Gen Zers Do Want to Buy Homes—They Just Can't Afford It, Even as Adults," CNBC, June 12, 2022, https://www.cnbc.com/2022/06/12/millennials-and-gen-zers-want-to-buy-homes-but-they-cant-afford-it.html.

In the aftermath of the COVID-19 epidemic, that was no sure bet, as scores of existing homeowners fanned out across the countryside, looking to scoop up or build new vacation homes in outlying areas.

As one might expect, this buying frenzy sent the value of residential real estate in many areas through the roof, causing some to worry that these inflated prices might cause renters to abandon the dream of homeownership altogether.

Subsequent studies have made it clear, however, that the vast majority of renters still aspire to become homeowners. According to one study, a whopping 73 percent of respondents cited homeownership as central to achieving the North American dream.

That's good news for everyone in the real estate business.

After all, change is one of the only constants in this business. Cities will keep evolving. Neighborhoods will rise and falter. New buildings will continue to be built. Existing properties will be renovated. And new plots and city lots will be developed.

Now, onto the slightly more disappointing news: according to some of the same data, nearly two-thirds of respondents said that inflated prices were preventing them from actually purchasing a new home.[8]

Respondents rattled off all the usual hurdles—insufficient income, inflated prices, and hefty down payments or closing costs—to explain why they worried they'd never be able to afford a home.[9]

Take note of that word—affordability—as I believe issues related to equity and opportunity are topics that we all avoid at our own peril.

Some might argue, of course, that there's nothing new under the sun. Younger families have long complained that they'd never amass

---

8   Annika Olson, "Millennials Have Almost No Chance of Being Able to Afford a House. This Is What Can Be Done," CNN, March 23, 2021, https://www.cnn.com/2021/03/23/opinions/millennials-almost-impossible-to-afford-home-olson/index.html.

9   Huddleston Jr., "Millennials and Gen Zers."

enough money to buy their own homes. Yet, over time, many manage to do so anyway.

The hard-hearted insist that low-income and middle-class renters will continue to do what they have always done: they'll keep on renting or head further outward from major metropolitan centers, beyond first-ring suburbs, and settle in the exurbs.

But what will happen if things really are different this time around? All one needs to do is peer across the Atlantic—to cities like London, Paris, Zurich, Geneva, and Munich—to see that the dream of homeownership in large urban areas already lies beyond the reach of millions of everyday Europeans.

Do we want the same thing to happen here, in Canada and North America?

I, for one, don't want to see that trend repeat itself here, especially since I built my business around helping renters become homeowners.

When real estate developers and agents simply shrug their shoulders at these problems, I can't help but think about my own upbringing.

One of the things I cherish most about the greater Toronto area is how diverse it is, including the fact that two hundred different languages continue to be spoken here.

Both of my grandfathers arrived in Canada as outsiders, yet they both found a way to assimilate into mainstream North American culture. They were different men, but they both bought and invested in real estate, settled in Richmond Hill, and used their properties to build wealth.

My paternal Italian-born grandfather settled in Richmond Hill when it was nothing more than a patch of dirt with some farmland sprinkled around it. In Italy his family lived in a mountaintop shack. Years later, after coming to Canada, he bought a house large enough to make all his family back in the old country go positively green with envy.

That's certainly progress. But if you judge your career purely on money alone, you're limiting your potential.

We can't allow future generations to believe that they won't be able to afford homes in the communities where they currently live.

I can't help but notice, for instance, the stunning rise in home prices where I live and feel a desire to use my standing in the industry to enact change. I'd argue, in fact, that my success is a direct result of me zeroing in on the need for revitalization rather than contributing to urban sprawl.

> **But if you judge your career purely on money alone, you're limiting your potential.**

So I ask you, as someone who's either in the industry or about to join it, what can we do to build and develop in a more responsible and equitable way?

One of the keys, I'd argue, lies in our willingness to embrace the core tenets of the new urbanism movement, which advocates for more intelligent growth and smarter development.

My entire business model is rooted in new urbanism, which goes by many names, including smart growth, intensification, or the new planning paradigm.

New urbanism argues against growth for growth's sake, reminding us that continued expansion into our green fields comes with potentially crippling environmental, social, and economic effects.

New urbanism inspires us to avoid these landmines by focusing on renovating the buildings we've already erected, the land we've already developed, and the cities we already call home. After all, some recent statistics show that there are a staggering 1.3 million vacant homes in Canada.[10]

Whenever I interview someone for a position in my company, I make sure to ask one very important question:

What motivates you to want to work in the real estate industry?

You'd be surprised how many candidates hem and haw—and stutter and stumble—when asked to describe what motivates them.

Some people are bluntly honest. It's all about the money, they'll tell me. They've met people who've made boatloads of money in real estate, and they figure they can do the same.

That's an honest response, I suppose, but not a particularly inspiring one, because, at the end of the day, you need to have passion and purpose to find true success in our field.

In fact I'd argue that we've come to a bit of a crossroads in regard to the real estate industry.

I think we must choose between two very different and divergent paths. The first one is relatively simple to follow. It looks safe and feels comforting, as it requires that we do nothing more than maintain the status quo.

Should we continue down this well-paved path, we will continue developing the same way we've been developing for the last seventy-five years—sweeping through and uprooting our precious native environments to make room for the next set of shiny new buildings and developments.

But we all know where this path will lead us, don't we? Not only are there environmental perils to destroying our precious fields and parkways, but we're also guaranteed to keep producing the very same soulless developments that are so prevalent today.

---

10   Stephen Punwasi, "New Data Shows Canada Still Has 1.3 Million Vacant Homes, Some Improvements Seen," Better Dwelling, February 16, 2022, https://better-dwelling.com/new-data-shows-canada-still-has-1-3-million-vacant-homes-some-improvements-seen/.

As the sprawl expands, ever outward, so too, I'd argue, will the distances between us. If new developments continue to be built, erasing more and more of what Mother Nature has so generously supplied us, we're going to feel even more divorced from nature (not to mention our neighbors) than we do at present.

Let's also not forget our dependency on automobiles—as well as some people's reticence to support public transit and ecologically conscious new infrastructure projects.

Simply put, our current direction is simply not sustainable in the long term.

Which brings us to the second path, which is far more jagged. In fact, it's a roadway that seems to bend slightly backward before jutting forward toward the horizon.

At first blush it looks like the more arduous path, but I believe, in the long run, it's the less perilous option. Why? Because it demands we take stock of where exactly we want to go as well as the *best* way to get there.

This path veers in a different direction from the first one—toward a future that prioritizes the revitalization of cities and the repurposing of underutilized and neglected buildings. It advocates for more walkable neighborhoods. Common-sense environmental standards. The introduction of more mixed-use and transit-oriented developments, in addition to a complete reevaluation of what the term "intensified built forms" means to all of us.

Should we select this path, we'll be required to restore and reawaken what already exists, while prioritizing the often-misunderstood concept of "community."

In short this second path calls for us to lean into the new urbanism movement, which has been my lodestar since the moment I entered the business in the mid-1990s.

Understanding New Urbanism

To understand the central tenets of new urbanism, first ask yourself this question: *Do I believe that each of us, in our own way, can help improve the communities in which we live and work?*

I think the response is fairly obvious, isn't it? We can all pitch in to improve our communities. Some will do so in small ways. Picking up trash. Volunteering at a local community center. Planting trees or beautifying sidewalks.

And others do so in more substantive ways by funding the creation of community centers. Launching nonprofits. Or running for public office.

I've already covered, in great detail, how you can do well for yourself by doing well for others—how a commitment to helping others generate real and lasting wealth puts you in a unique position to do the same for yourself.

Now, let me describe, as best I can, how adopting a new-urbanism mindset can extend that virtuous cycle even further—dramatically improving the cities and communities where you work, while simultaneously helping you generate wealth in the process.

I'm a developer, so I realize that every new building that gets built is a minor miracle. But at the same time, wouldn't you agree that some developments are slightly more miraculous than others?

I've come to realize that being a developer isn't like playing Monopoly. We shouldn't strive to wantonly fill the entire board, to build on every single lot, from Park Place to Connecticut Avenue, that we happen to land on.

In the end, quality should trump quantity.

Which is one of the reasons why I'm so drawn to new urbanism. It's both a practical and philosophical movement. It encourages us to look backward—at the way we used to live—so that we can sprint forward with a greater sense of purpose toward the way we should be living.

In a more pragmatic sense, adopting a new-urbanism mindset is simply a smart business decision. When you use new urbanism as a guide, you're more likely to invest in the right kinds of properties and develop the kind of projects that local officials and planning boards can't help but support and approve.

I guarantee you this: the more you study the tenets of new urbanism, the more you'll understand why today's current zoning bylaws, provincial policies, and official plans were written the way they were.

I'd argue that it's going to be virtually impossible to be a successful real estate agent or developer in the years ahead if you fail to embrace the new urbanism movement, because it's going to dominate urban planning for decades to come.

I was first introduced to the movement in the early 2000s. Shortly after I completed my first development, my lawyer at the time, Ron Kanter, invited me to attend an urban-planning symposium being held in the city of Markham, Ontario.

Residents and city officials living in Markham were abuzz over the completion of a new "community village" called Cornell. During the late 1990s, many viewed the development as something of an experiment, an attempt to build a self-sustained community where residents could conveniently live, play, and shop in one place.

The community included an array of detached and semidetached homes, plenty of green space, walkable boulevards, ample bike lanes, and a quaint town square. It was, in short, a throwback to the way Canadians used to live and was, arguably, the first neighborhood in Toronto built with the new urbanism movement specifically in mind.

I was immediately drawn to what I saw there. It struck me as an ideal template for urban living. Distinctive architecture. Plenty of parks. Pedestrian-friendly streetscapes, all of which encouraged people to get out of their homes and interact with each other the way Europeans live and have lived for centuries.

While attending the symposium, I remember the mayor of Markham, Don Cousens, saying, "This symposium is about a development movement whose main purpose is to bring people together!" It was such a simple phrase—bring people together—but ultimately a powerful one for me personally.

I remember thinking to myself, "Now, here's a movement that I can believe in, one committed to ushering in a future that's worth fighting for."

After all, I'm a very visual person. Some people can only see the buildings, corners, and communities as they currently exist. By contrast I've always possessed an ability to see what could be, which is a prerequisite for anyone interested in new urbanism.

After all, new urbanism asks us all to consider what we've lost and what we've gained, in terms of urban planning, since World War II.

Close your eyes, and unlock your imagination for a moment: if you could somehow slip back in time, perhaps to the late nineteenth or early twentieth century, you'd probably notice that most towns and municipalities were built around centralized hubs (town squares), which radiated outward in every direction via walkable paths and open lanes.

As a result most residents lived, worked, socialized, shopped, and celebrated together in close proximity to one other. Public spaces were truly public, thus encouraging people with different jobs and incomes to interact with one another on a daily basis.

As a result this classical approach to urban planning required a plethora of mixed-use buildings as well as the continual revitalization of existing structures, as opposed to the construction of new communities on the fields and along the streams beyond the city's borders.

Consider how much the principles of urban planning have shifted since then. Think about the emphasis that we've placed on highways and cars and low-density developments.

Think of the endless expanse of gated communities, cul-de-sacs, and single-family homes that have sprouted up since then. Consider how this expansion from city centers has changed our lives, including how vehicular traffic is prioritized over other modes of urban transportation, whether it's walking, bicycling, or public transportation.

Life, as a result, has become more fragmented, producing disconnected fiefdoms. If anything, we seemed to have moved further away from each other with each subsequent generation.

It's worth noting that it's not so much that the old ways were ideal, but rather that the pendulum may have swung too far in one direction.

New urbanism does not advocate, as some have argued, that we move backward. It doesn't champion regression. Nor does it seek to halt growth of new developments. Rather, it seeks to promote smarter and more responsible developments.

When I think about new urbanism, for instance, I can't help but think about my father, as the movement has always relied on visionaries to transform its bold ideas into brick-and-mortar realities. In short it requires developers, true risk-takers and problem solvers, who know how to make things happen.

For me, my father was one of those visionaries. He specialized in something we refer to in the business as back lotting. In essence he'd gather together dozens of property owners—sometimes as many as forty intensely opinionated Italian gentlemen—into one room and try to get them all to agree to work together to develop a road in their backyards. This would essentially allow each property owner to sever off half of his lot into two lots: with one lot fronting onto the new road and his existing lot fronting onto the existing street.

It was complicated work. To me it felt a little bit like trying to herd forty feral cats into one really small barn. But in most cases, he succeeded in getting everyone on the same page, which benefited both the owners of the land and the community itself. So much so that there's a street in Richmond Hill that's named after our family. It's called Arten Avenue.

My father became an expert in infill developments long before the new urbanism movement gained momentum in the mid-1990s. He understands land severances, options on properties, back lotting, townhomes, and how to create more practical lots in run-down areas better than most.

The revitalization of communities in Richmond Hill, especially on Benson and Hall and Hunt Avenues, where I completed four midsize developments, was started by my father. It was a neighborhood once known as a safe haven for Hells Angels biker gangs.

My father had the vision to help transform this once-run-down neighborhood into a truly desirable destination. In fact he completed the first change-of-use townhome development there.

Many new developers, including me, and property owners soon followed his lead, and in time it became a beautiful neighborhood filled with high-end townhomes. Now that area is, without question, one of the most stunning areas to live in greater Toronto.

New urbanists, like me, want to build on those efforts and support the renaissance of human-scale neigh-

> **Call me idealistic, but I wholeheartedly believe that the quality of the buildings, homes, and developments in our neighborhoods has a profound impact on our ability to live happy and prosperous lives.**

borhoods. We want to use existing tools to explore how zoning laws, traffic flow patterns, and underutilized buildings can be readapted to bolster the economic and environmental health of our communities.

In essence we want to use our buildings to bring people back together, both in downtown metropolitan areas as well as suburban communities.

It's a pragmatic movement, which argues that we can reclaim and beautify what we've already built, while we simultaneously lean into daring new ideas on how to drive down costs and provide renters greater opportunities to become homeowners.

New urbanism asks us to reconsider what a good redevelopment project looks like. Can we, as developers, improve on existing buildings by connecting them with public transportation? Can we challenge ourselves to build vibrant, eco-friendly buildings that draw people together and restore a sense of shared ownership and community?

Call me idealistic, but I wholeheartedly believe that the quality of the buildings, homes, and developments in our neighborhoods has a profound impact on our ability to live happy and prosperous lives.

New urbanism also appeals to me because it demands collaboration between different communities. It applies healthy pressure to developers and real estate professionals, while inviting contributions from architects, local residents, urban planners, engineers, and local interest groups who already live in these towns and cities.

It's a call to action that argues it's possible for us all to move forward by adopting a "back to the future" mentality, especially when it comes to environmental concerns.

Not an idealistic soul? Okay, let's be practical then: local governments across North America have made it clear that they have no interest in allowing developers to continue paving over green spaces and developing projects on once-fertile tracts of farmland.

Thus, I'd argue that understanding—and adopting—a new urbanism mindset simply makes good business sense, as its tenets are quickly becoming prerequisites for anyone who wants to be a developer or real estate professional in North America.

So why not sit down, learn more about the movement, and try to extract your own personal purpose from its tenets now, rather than when it's too late in the game?

I've spoken a great deal in this book about the importance of providing clients what I've described as the "ultimate service." And to my mind, new urbanism is simply an extension of that same idea.

New urbanism is a means for all of us to render a service to our communities. It addresses, in a very logical way, how we can continue building and developing with stewardship, equity, and responsibility in mind.

It's the answer, in my opinion, to the question, "How can we do our jobs while simultaneously ensuring that the dream of homeownership remains alive and well for the next generation?"

I'd argue that every project we've discussed over the course of this book is, in one form or another, a prime example of new urbanism in action.

If you take a sparsely populated area that contains a handful of homes and turn it into a condo or townhome development, that's a new urbanism project. If you help a family renovate their basement into a rentable space, that's new urbanism. If you change the use of an existing property to bolster density in an area, that's new urbanism.

But let me offer another anecdote from my own portfolio as evidence of new urbanism in action.

In 2011 I purchased a building from a very good friend of mine, Lou Kelly, in Barrie, Ontario, which is approximately ninety kilometers north of Toronto. At the time, he was running one of the largest HomeLife real estate offices outside of the greater Toronto area, which consisted of roughly sixty-five Realtors. Nonetheless, he wanted out. So, he sold me the building and his business and went on to his next adventure.

At the time rumors had begun to swirl that his land might be expropriated by the community to build a new road. It was nothing more than idle speculation at the time, but if these plans did move forward, I knew it would dramatically change the value of the property.

If things did progress, I would be buying a valuable property right off Highway 400. Everyone who drove up to their vacation homes in Muskoka and Georgian Bay on the weekends would pass my intersection.

Suffice to say I saw the possibilities of what might be, so I bought the parcel and business for $1 million. Lou gave me very good terms on the brokerage, and we sealed the deal.

After renovating the building, I used it as an office. Then, in 2016, I bought two properties behind my new office for $200,000 each.

And sure enough, in 2020, those long-gestating plans to widen the road and build a new ramp onto Highway 400 began to take shape. The rumors were finally becoming a reality. The Ministry of Transportation needed my land to build the new thoroughfare. Nevertheless, I stayed the course. I argued that they should expropriate the land in a way that took over a portion of my land but preserved the existing building.

Meanwhile, I developed plans to build a sixteen-story building on the site. As of this writing, I'm very close to securing a positive planning report on that proposal.

We have a very strong case. Besides, the Ministry of Transportation doesn't oppose the development; they just want to seize the land without giving me full market value.

If the project is approved, my building will stand as a classic example of new urbanism in action. Why? Because there's a dire need for more rental units in Barrie, as the town borders Sheridan College.

This building, which will be strategically placed near a major highway, will supply much-needed affordable rental units, while bringing people together to generate a sense of community. It's a classic intensified built form, which uses land that once held a commercial building and two houses. Our initial pro forma has the building worth $90 million when built and leased out from an income approach. Affordable housing? Ninety million dollars? Change the use, folks! New urbanism is good business!

My advice to you: follow our lead and harness your passion by prioritizing a greater purpose, as I have.

By all means think like a salesperson. Think like an entrepreneur. Be a mentor. Be a real estate agent. Be a developer. You can do all the above while thinking like a shrewd urban planner.

Wade deep into the sort of topics—infrastructure, sewers, zoning, environmental stewardship—that most people don't have the time or inclination to think about. Think big and think small. Think short term and long term. And you'll be rewarded.

I know, for instance, that my wife and I are better for it. For one day, years from now, when our children and grandchildren gather around our dinner table and ask us what we did for a living, we'll not only be able to tell them what we did, but we'll also be able to break down why we did it.

We'll be able to describe what we achieved. How we reinvigorated communities across greater Toronto. How we went the extra mile to help low- and middle-income renters become first-time homebuyers. How we helped clients transform partially finished basements into income-generating rental units. How we bought small, sparsely populated lots of land and transformed them into massive townhomes and towering condominium complexes that housed thousands of people. How we played a role in pumping life and commerce into corner lots that were once overlooked and underused. And how we helped breathe new life into communities like the 163 condo community Riverside Suites in Old Weston of Toronto, the Dogpatch in Newmarket, Bikers Haven on Benson and Hall, and Hunt Avenue in Richmond Hill, and the much needed sixteen-story rental community in Barrie.

In short I hope you'll be able to say, when retirement beckons, that you didn't just sell houses, or work for a sales team, or spend your career trying to massage your fragile ego. Or worst of all that you spent all your time trying to build an elegant downline. What I hope you'll be able to say is that you did your best to build and develop stronger, more vibrant communities. That you tried to make a difference in people's lives. That you offered an ultimate service to your clients, supported worthwhile change-of-use projects, and embraced the tenets of new urbanism.

In short, that you led with purpose.

Oh, and the money? The money, I promise you, will come if you subscribe to these principles. Do things the right way for the right reason, and you'll achieve a level of wealth far greater than anything you could have thought possible.

CHAPTER 9

MY REAL ESTATE COMMANDMENTS:
TIMELESS ADVICE FOR A TIMELESS PROFESSION

W hen I was in the twelfth grade, I read a novel called *The Appren-ticeship of Duddy Kravitz*, which had a profound effect on my life and future career.

I'm not sure people read the book as much now as people did when I was younger, but it remains, in my eyes, one of the most interesting—and instructive—novels about the real estate profession I've ever read.

Back in 1974, Hollywood made a film adaption of the novel, which starred Richard Dreyfus, Randy Quaid, and Jack Warden. But in my opinion, the movie can't hold a candle to the original book.

I remember our teacher, Mrs. Heslip, picking up a piece of chalk one morning and scrawling Duddy's name across her chalkboard. There was something about that name—Duddy Kravitz—that imme-diately grabbed my attention.

The character of Duddy Kravitz sprang from the imagination of well-respected Canadian author Mordecai Richler back in 1959.

When we were assigned to read about Duddy, I'm sure most of my classmates yawned, writing it off as the latest entry in a long line of boring reading assignments. Only it turned out to be much more than homework to me.

The book follows the aforementioned Duddy Kravitz, a driven young entrepreneur who becomes obsessed with three things: money, prestige, and quality real estate.

Early in the book, Duddy is presented as a sympathetic character. He's a poor kid from Montreal who lives with a dysfunctional family that shuns him in favor of his brother, who's determined to be a famous doctor.

Over the course of the book, Duddy proves to be every bit as driven as his brother. He dedicates himself to making a name for himself, even if he's initially unsure how to transcend his humble beginnings.

I remember opening the book and immediately falling under its spell. I just couldn't put it down. For some reason Duddy's life and his upbringing, while different from my own, resonated with me from the jump.

I felt completely swept away by the adventure of it all. Duddy's journey felt like an action-packed career worth pursuing.

I loved what he did every day. The negotiations. The deals. The buildings. His personal love story. And all the drama he encountered along the way.

Here was a book, I quickly realized, that explored the complexities of the immigrant experience through the very specific lens of buying, developing, and selling real estate.

So, I settled in, flopping onto my bed that first night, and started riffling through pages. Page one. Page two. Page ten. Page twenty-two. Page thirty-one. I couldn't put the book down, because it felt like an honest account of what could happen to someone like me in the years to come.

Say what you will about the semiacerbic way Richler presents Duddy in the book. But Duddy Kravitz is no cookie-cutter character.

He's certainly flawed, yet an undeniably three-dimensional character. He's the kind of guy, God bless him, who's not afraid to chase after his dreams—someone who won't settle, no matter the circumstances, for what most people would describe as an "ordinary life."

He's a grinder. A real worker bee. No job is too big, and no job is too small, which I think we can all admire.

The problem, at least early in the book, is that he can't quite figure out what he should be working toward or be passionate about.

One line, for better or for worse, has never left me. It's seared into my consciousness like a seal pressed into hot wax. *A man without land is nobody.*

That line is initially spoken by Duddy's grandfather, who can tell that Duddy has ambition but lacks direction. So he calls young Duddy to his side and lets him in on what he considered to be a pearl of true wisdom: "A man without land," grandfather tells Duddy, "is nobody."

Duddy soaks up his grandfather's advice in one glorious gulp. He discovers his purpose, right there, in that moment. Real estate, he decrees, is going to be the key to transforming himself from anonymity into respected businessman.

As you might've guessed, Duddy goes out into the world and finds that reconciling his dreams with reality of the real world isn't as easy as it sounds.

As the story progresses, we realize that Duddy's perpetually over-inflated ego is slowly evolving into his tragic flaw.

He experiences more than his fair share of triumphs and setbacks along the way, both personally and professionally. As the plot progresses, Duddy's imperfections become magnified with each passing page, to the point where we, as readers, are asked to render a judgment as to whether everything Duddy has sacrificed is worth the price he seems willing to pay.

I'm no literature critic. I have no desire to wade into the politics or the critiques that have been leveled against the book over the years. Or even render a final judgment on Duddy himself.

All I can tell you is that, back in the twelfth grade, that book whisked me away into a fantastic world filled with unique characters and unexpected plot twists.

Truth be told, I'm very different from the fictional character of Duddy Kravitz—except perhaps in two important ways.

No. 1: I was then, and continue to this day to be, magnetically drawn to the great big carnival that is the real estate profession.

And No. 2: I will always retain a soft spot in my heart for people who dream big rather than settle for quotidian aspirations.

Like Duddy I sincerely love my work. The planning. The financing. The collaboration. The renovation. The selling. The buying. The closings. The openings. The land. And most importantly the countless number of clients and partners I've worked with over the years.

A life spent in real estate, in my opinion, will teach you more about life than any other career path you can choose. But what I've tried to do, in sitting down to write this book, is to prove to you that real estate is one of the few businesses in this world where you can start with virtually nothing and end up with more wealth and wisdom than you could ever imagine.

The problem, of course, is that you need to stick with it—through the rough spots and the stressful nights—to reap all the rewards it can bestow upon you. You need, as I've mentioned throughout this book, to display a level of tenacity and stick-to-itiveness that many of your peers won't be able to achieve.

It bothers me, for example, to see so many talented young real estate agents abandon their practices within five years of launching them. Some surveys indicate that the dropout rate for real estate agents might be as high as 85 percent for the first five years they're in the business.[11]

What sours so many people, I often wonder, about a profession that's been such a blessing for me and so many of my peers?

There are plenty of practical reasons, I suppose, why people leave. Some simply don't have the interpersonal skills to connect with people. Others are incapable of putting in the hustle and hard work needed to achieve—and maintain—long-term success. Others struggle to generate enough leads or wind up partnering with the wrong broker at the start of their careers.

Which is why we do things differently at TREC. As cliché as it sounds, we view our agents as members of our extended family. We train our Realtors. We point out the potential pitfalls that we've experienced during our journeys, all while encouraging them to grow not only in their jobs but also as real estate professionals.

One of the things we guarantee our people is that we'll give them all the support, advice, and tools needed for them to climb as high as possible. Everyone in our office is sincere when we say that we're invested in their success.

I point this out because far too many real estate professionals opt to leave the business because they tire of performing the same rote duties and responsibilities, year after year. After a while, if you don't grow professionally, you grow personally resentful.

> **After a while, if you don't grow professionally, you grow personally resentful.**

Buyers' agents, especially, tend to get stuck on a never-ending merry-go-round of open houses and

11   Tom Ferry, "Why Most Real Estate Agents Fail," November 15, 2021, https://www.tomferry.com/blog/87-of-all-agents-fail-in-real-estate/.

demanding clients. I hope, by reading this book, that you recognize how many different opportunities are out there for you, if you only expend the time and energy to reach out and grab them.

Personally, I'm never bored. For me every single day is as unpredictable as it is stimulating. Every project is an adventure. Every client meeting is an opportunity to do and learn something new about my community and the people who live within it.

But here's the thing: over the last three-plus decades, I can honestly say I've never experienced a single dull day, because I made it a priority to build a diversified portfolio of businesses.

I didn't allow myself to get bored, because I kept expanding my sphere of interests.

I continue to help buyers and sellers, as I did in my early years, but now I buy and renovate properties too. I still help people finance large and small homes, but now I buy and develop—hold and sell—my own properties as well.

I do it all. And I sincerely hope, if you take one thing from my journey, it's that you can do the same. The only thing preventing you from finding success is the little voice in your head that whispers, "I can't do it; it's just too risky."

Variety is the spice of life, right? So why not think like an entrepreneur and branch out beyond your comfort zones? Go out there and build your business vertically as well as horizontally.

Remember that real estate is a tangible asset. You can own it. Buy it. Flip it. Renovate it. Finance it. Change its use. Lend money against it.

I could go on and on in regard to the nearly infinite number of things you can do working in the real estate field.

So why not roll up your sleeves and do it all—or at the very least do more than what you're currently doing right now? After all, you happen to be holding the secret recipe for success at this very moment.

Here's the road map as I've tried to draw it for you. Maybe you're at the beginning of this journey. Maybe you're somewhere in the middle. Doesn't matter. Here's what you have to do:

Step one: Start out by representing buyers. Learn how the buying process works. Study different financing options. Recognize the value of changing the use of existing properties.

In short, learn the art of making money when you buy real estate.

Step two: At some point, go out, take what you've learned, and start investing in properties yourself. Start small if you have to. Spruce up and renovate your own house. Buy a condo you can lease. Renovate a basement and rent it out. Turn a three-bedroom home into a four-bedroom rental. Buy a home for your principal residence. Live in it. Remodel it. Change its use. Sell it, and move onto the next one. Each successful deal will put you in a better position to execute bigger deals down the road.

Work all the angles, especially when it comes to funding and financing. Then, bundle up what you've learned, share all the wisdom you've acquired, and recycle it back to your clients so that they can continue climbing too.

Step three: Keep expanding your business prospects. Make it a priority to launch and spin off new businesses if you can. Take your pick: A renovation business. A development management business. A building business. A lending business. Try something new so that you can generate multiple revenue streams. And make sure to systemize your operation so that you can continue growing.

Step four: Buy additional real estate, and do your best to hold on to it. The key to a developer's success is staying power. When you buy real estate and take on additional mortgages, you get into the habit of investing money into your properties, which is always money well spent.

Remember: waste not, want not. Don't waste precious capital. Stay focused on your real estate business plan. My first car was a Honda Accord. I drove that car for years, even while I was amassing a treasure trove of valuable real estate.

Step five: Take baby steps toward developing your own small (then medium and finally large-scale) development projects. Hold some; sell others. Bank it all, and then start the process all over again—rinse, wash, repeat—knowing you can become a little more ambitious every time.

Trust me when I tell you, if you follow the above recipe, boredom won't be part of your vocabulary.

After all, success is predicated on building more than just a sales practice. It demands you take a more holistic view of all the opportunities that the real estate world can afford you.

I hate to go all Tony Robbins on you at the close, but 50 percent of success in this business derives from adopting the right mindset. The other half comes from following through on your dreams and executing, executing, executing.

In order to execute, you need to be willing to take risks. So make your move. Now.

Sometimes, you're going to fall flat on your face. But in other instances, you're going to beat the odds. The key is to live with both experiences—the setbacks and the triumphs—just the same.

As I constantly tell our agents at TREC, we can all learn a lot from the Apple corporation.

Why is Apple so successful, year in and year out, decade after decade? How does Apple consistently exceed its previous sales records?

By continually introducing new products that people want to buy and offering their customers a level of service that's better than what anyone else in their space can provide.

Think last year's iPhone was impressive? says Apple CEO Tim Cook. Let me introduce you to our newest model. Been using the same ear buds for the last three decades? Look at these nifty new AirPods!

Take a moment to consider the dizzying number of products that Apple has added to its catalog over the last decade or so. iPads. Apple Watches. New iMacs. Not to mention all their new services: Apple Plus. Apple Music. Apple Fitness. Apple Arcade and so on.

What are some of the key lessons that we, as real estate agents and developers, need to take from Apple's success? Here's the short answer: we can excel by diversifying our offerings and our skill sets, and we need to be willing to pivot on a dime when the circumstances call for it.

Scared of the prospect of taking on another major development project? Fine. Don't do it. Take on what you can handle. Create something new. Launch new products that will broaden your business. Offer a different set of services. Stay limber, and keep those creative juices flowing. Don't be robotic.

The beauty of this profession is that (a) there are so many opportunities to be creative and (b) the most successful real estate professionals are invariably the most creative thinkers.

Build your career on that bedrock principle, and I guarantee you that you'll exceed even your loftiest expectations. And on top of it, you're going to feel good about the career decisions you've made. Your career is going to be more rewarding than the folks who chose to be stockbrokers or financial advisors, because the quality and excitement of your life will outshine theirs.

You'll experience more thrills, more freedom, and more creativity in five years than they'll experience in a lifetime.

That's the core message I want to leave you with. Dream big dreams. Don't settle. Don't allow yourself, as Duddy Kravitz teaches us, to get bored or distracted or hoodwinked by people who put their own interests ahead of your own.

I'm a big believer, as I hope I've demonstrated, in breaking down complex ideas into simple, bite-sized nuggets.

I wanted this book to be substantive, not rhetorical puffery. I wanted it to delve into philosophical arguments while offering practical solutions. I wanted to give you advice that could bolster your career—wisdom that was simultaneously referential and inspirational. Lessons that you could turn to in times of need to remind you that there were better days ahead. In short, a book that reminded you there are plenty of opportunities that lay before you, just waiting to be collected.

So, what better way to close our time together than by sharing with you a set of commandments that have guided me in my career—and rules that have the potential to benefit you in your travels? These are my real rules for real success. I hope that they help you grow and that you, in turn, pay things forward, by creating your own commandments and sharing them with others in the years to come.

Don't Be Hoodwinked by Slick Recruitment Pitches

Nothing angers me more than to see good real estate agents get bamboozled by slick recruiting ploys and empty marketing pitches. I think I've made it abundantly clear how futile it is to follow anyone who prattles on about teams and downlines as well as people who boast that they have "the most market share in the entire industry."

So let me give it to you straight: they're lying to you. "Market share" is a term that's thrown around a lot in other industries but is practically meaningless in the real estate world.

My advice? Whenever someone slips you one of those tired real estate pickup lines, make them explain themselves. Ask your potential employer or colleague or motivational speaker what they mean when they say they have amassed the most market share, or are the top broker or sales representative in the state, or assembled the highest-ranking team, or built the ultimate downline.

Here's the truth: if you have access to the MLS, you have access to the exact same properties as everyone else. Every professional real estate agent possesses the same market share. In case you haven't noticed, there are no pay walls on the MLS. And there's only one MLS. We all see the exact same listings; therefore, we all have access to the exact same properties. So, what does market share mean exactly?

Answer: nothing.

It's All about Location, Location, Location

The same goes for any broker who goes around saying that they're somehow better equipped to represent buyers and sellers in a given neighborhood because they've been working in the area longer than you have.

No one owns a street, a neighborhood, or a city. Smart real estate agents help outsiders become the new pillars of established neighborhoods. So be a conduit for change, and don't let anyone scare you into thinking their history is more powerful than your drive.

At the end of the day, it's about providing the ultimate service to your clients. All clients want to know is what you can do for them. So work hard to cultivate the right mindset, one that will help you generate real wealth for your clients and ultimately for yourself. Your clients are paying for your experience and your skill sets. Nothing more, nothing less.

I'm a proud Canadian, and I'm proud that I've lived in greater Toronto my whole life, but the fact that I've worked with clients, investors, and real estate agents across North America and Europe has only benefited me over the years. I don't see any advantage whatsoever in being a provincial-minded broker.

I've learned a great deal about this business by leaving my own home turf and talking to buyers, sellers, and real estate professionals around the globe. In fact I think that developing friendships and contacts around the world is an advantage, as those interactions gave me advance warning as to how international or regional market trends might impact us here in Canada.

It all comes down to this: at the end of the day, you're not so much partnering with a brand as you're partnering with your broker. So choose wisely. Align yourself with someone who has your best interests at heart, rather than their own.

Remember These Three Words: Change the Use

There's a phenomenon in major league baseball called "playing small ball." In contrast to playing "long ball," which encourages players to do everything in their power to hit home runs, "small ball" argues that a team can score just as many runs by getting guys on base, moving them into scoring position, and bringing them home with singles, bunts, and sacrifice flies.

In baseball, as in real estate, everyone wants to hit home runs. Everyone wants the big score. People want to generate tons of cash in a very short period of time. The problem, of course, is that most people strike out before they can ever close the big deals they're chasing.

By this point it should be abundantly clear to you that there's great value to be found in changing the use of existing structures. If you have the expertise and financing acumen to convert a lot with two houses on it into a twenty-story building, do it. But there's plenty of wealth to be generated by taking on the smaller projects and doing all the little things correctly.

If you have an opportunity to add a bedroom so that you (or the property's owners) can rent out the extra space and bring in an additional income stream—do it. If you have the opportunity to convert a half-finished basement into a rentable space—do it. If you can find a way to rent out a portion of your home to help pay for an expansion or renovation—do it.

Each time you seize upon these opportunities, you will develop the tools and expertise to change the use of real estate. If you start small, it'll allow you to hit some monster home-run deals later.

After all, real estate, like baseball, is about maintaining the right momentum. You need to keep inching forward. Keep stringing together enough hits—that is, profitable projects—and you're ultimately going to win the game.

As a real estate agent or developer, you don't have to be the biggest and the best on the block. You just have to make the most of the land, properties, and buildings that are available to you.

Be creative. Think outside the box. Work on envisioning what a piece of real estate can become for you and your clients. This will jump-start your creativity. There are always better opportunities and value in resale than in new construction, for as my father taught me at a very young age, your biggest gains in real estate come when you change the use.

Tenacity Wins: Always Play Like You're Behind

When times are tough, you have to find the strength to keep battling. It's no different from when your favorite hockey team is locked in a tight playoff game. Some teams cave, and some rise to the occasion.

As someone who loves and coaches hockey teams, I refer to this do-or-die mindset as "playing desperate hockey."

All things being equal, it's usually the team that wants it more that takes home the win. Ditto for real estate agents and developers.

Good week? Good month? Good year?

> ## Good week? Good month? Good year? Good for you, but don't you dare take it for granted.

Good for you, but don't you dare take it for granted.

Instead, ask yourself this question: Am I working like I'm behind by two goals, or am I skating like I have a three-goal lead?

Better to play desperate hockey, even if you find yourself enjoying a hot streak. Why? Because real estate is a business dominated by headstrong people.

Everyone has a job to do, but the question to ask is this: Who's capable of performing those jobs better than the person next to them?

You control your own destiny. Forget about your competition. It's your responsibility to flip the switch and make it happen when an opportunity presents itself. The real estate market has tanked? A project is in peril? A client has left you out to dry? Experiencing family troubles?

Work through them. Be resilient.

You can make more money in a down market than a booming one. In fact the best opportunities of my career came during down markets. So stand ready to change your business plan on a dime. When markets are down, that's the time to buy. So, if you focus on creating wealth on the buyer side, you will flourish in down markets far more than the competition will.

I often say that the best developers, real estate investors, and real estate professionals are warriors. You need to develop character and have sticking power. You need to be able to compartmentalize everything and occasionally kick things into a higher gear.

So skate harder. Want it more than the other guys. If you're at your best during moments of crisis, chances are you'll be the one lifting the cup at the close of it all.

Biggest Gains Come When You Build Something from Nothing

Humility is underrated. Over the course of my career, I've worked with paupers and princes. Clients who had empty bank accounts and clients who had more money than they knew what to do with. And I did my best to treat them both exactly the same.

Why? Because people who have very little—and therefore have everything to lose if things go south—tend to appreciate other people's help more than those who don't really need it.

In my experience renters and working-class folks rarely forget a kind act, especially when it comes from a real estate agent. They'll not only pay things forward, but they'll also pay you back tenfold with referrals and loyalty for decades thereafter.

In short they'll remember you and what you did for them. They'll keep dancing, as the old saying says, "with the one who brought them."

So, when they rise, you'll rise. When they need to trade up for a new home or a second home, they'll call you to represent them. They'll ask for you by name because you helped them when so many others wouldn't give them the time of day.

Whenever I'm asked how I catapulted into the top 1 percent of agents in Canada in less than three years, I tell people, "Good clients." And I mean that sincerely. The best bets you can make in life are the ones you place on yourself and hardworking folks who are committed to making a better life for themselves and their families.

Oh, and let's not forget the bigger picture. When you help families turn nothing into something, you can create real wealth for them and yourself. You'll look at real estate differently and begin focusing on how you can make money buying real estate.

Listing homes is certainly a major component of our business and shouldn't be ignored. However, the bigger play lies in building a real estate empire.

Having assisted numerous families in pursuing their dreams, I learned how to finance real estate, how to oversee the change-of-use process, and how to work with renovators, banks, urban planners, engineers, municipal lawyers, city officials, councillors, builders, and developers, all of whom helped me to become the developer I am today.

Less Ego, More Wealth Creation

At some point in your career, you're going to have to ask yourself, "What's more important to me, wealth or fame?"

Do you want to feed your ego or build your net worth?

Maybe, in Hollywood, these aren't binary choices. You see plenty of stars who become wealthy by doing everything in their power to stroke their own egos. The same principle doesn't apply, however, to real estate, as too many people in our line of work fall prey to the hype instead of putting in the hard work.

In this business, inflated egos kill more careers than bad deals. Strong work ethic? Passion and drive? High risk tolerance? Those are essential building blocks for success. But for a whole bunch of people, success isn't enough. They crave fame.

They'll fork over ridiculous amounts of money to plaster their faces across billboards and bus stops. Before you know it, all that attention becomes so addictive that they'll do and say anything to stay in the spotlight.

So I beg you, for your own good: avoid partnering with brokers and partners who are addicted to fame. They won't help you, because, invariably, they'll want to prop themselves up by using you as a step stool for further self-aggrandizement.

Don't let them do it. Don't let them use you and discard you. When your broker starts to prioritize their ego over your success, just dump 'em. Walk away, because real wealth is invisible, not flashy.

The flashy folks don't tend to have as much wealth as they claim they do. More often than not, true wealth is what you can't see. How does that old saying go? New money flaunts it; smart money keeps it.

So, when you pick a partner or join a brokerage, do your homework. Ignore the window dressing. Ask your potential employer to show you what's really underneath the hood of their operation. People who've accomplished something of note won't squirm when they're asked to prove their worth and wisdom.

Make sure your brokers can prove they are as skilled and successful as they claim to be. It's best to trust but verify, as a good broker will support you; a corrupt one will decimate your career.

Don't be fooled by the fake numbers or the fancy offices or all the vapid hype that comes with it. There are plenty of people in this business who will manipulate numbers to their advantage and relish in making smooth-sounding but ultimately empty claims.

So do your research. Study neighborhoods and official planning documents. Explore where future rapid transportation stations will be established. Play the long game: buy the worst house on the street in the best location. Devise strategies to help finance your clients' needs, which will in turn help you finance your own real estate portfolio.

Cash (Flow) Is King

I won't belabor a point I've already made a dozen times in a dozen different ways: in this business you can't afford to have your cash flow tied to your equity. You just can't do it. It's not a venial transgression; it's a cardinal sin that's sunk more people than I can count.

I know that we all want to hold on to what we've built, and there is no question that holding on to valuable properties has proven to be the best strategy for wealth creation. Sometimes, however, you have to sell one development and turn your capital over so that you can move onto the next development.

Onward and upward. It's that simple. Sometimes, as the gambler tells us, you gotta know when to hold 'em and know when to fold 'em.

Throughout my career I've made sure to keep money flowing into my coffers by diversifying my businesses and services. I continue to work with buyers, large and small, to earn commissions. I ran a renovation business for years. So, yes, location, location, location is critical. But so is diversification, diversification, diversification.

There is only so much money you can make in sales. You need to systemize your operation so that you can focus on building additional revenue streams, like the project management as well as the renovation work.

That being said, keep your eyes peeled for quality prospects. Make sure to share your love of real estate with both buyers and sellers. Your passion has to shine through. Remember when you diversify and a shovel goes in the ground and financing kicks in on one of your projects, small or large. Then, *cha-ching*—you've got cash flow!

Don't be afraid to set aside your pride and rent out your basement or office or your garage. I've done all the above. I am definitely my mother's son in this regard! I created the cash flow and kept my eyes on long-term plays, just as you should.

Always Remember That Real Estate Is a People Business

Learning how to leverage social media has extraordinary value in our business. Doesn't matter if you're an agent, developer, buyer, or seller, we all rely on social media in one way or another. At TREC we have an automated social media platform that generates and posts content, from marketing reports to breaking updates, every single day.

As such, social media is invaluable for reminding current and potential clients that you're available to help them. But let's keep things real, shall we? Social media is not going to determine whether you succeed or fail, whether you flame out in a few years or generate more wealth than you've ever dreamed of.

You can post all the dynamic content you like. But social media is not a surrogate for old-school face-to-face or voice-to-voice communication.

As I've already said, people buy with their emotions and justify with logic. And enthusiasm is the key to being persuasive without being pushy. If you think that you can generate as much emotion with a tweet as a phone call, you're sadly mistaken.

Social media breeds awareness. Interpersonal relationships close deals. And don't let anyone else tell you otherwise. So pick up your phone and call your clients. Call your leads. Don't be passive. Be enthusiastic. Prove to them that you're more than a glorified robot who can send texts.

One of my valuable skill sets is my ability to build rapport with people. I am my father's son in this respect!

Building a Client-Engagement Plan— Credibility Is Everything

If you're not succeeding in this business, it's because you haven't built a solid database. If you want to be successful, you need to touch your database every ten days. No exceptions. Always keep in contact with your clients.

You can do so in a variety of ways. Quarterly newsletters. Market reports. Personal visits. Gift cards. Holiday cards. Personal text messages to commemorate key anniversaries. Personal shout-outs with videos on their birthdays.

> If you're not succeeding in this business, it's because you haven't built a solid database.

My favorite client-appreciation gift is a set of Cutco knives, which is near and dear to my heart, as this is where I learned and developed my sales experience.

Find your own special gift, and send it. I once sent out blankets that had the names of clients' family members embroidered on them. I guarantee you some of my clients are still snuggling up with those blankets to this day.

As I've already noted, I'm not a big fan of working in teams. When you work in teams, you tend to lose sight of this personal touch. While it is an efficient system of sales volume, I don't believe teams allow you to forge a personal connection with clients.

The two components I can add to this list are credibility and follow-through. There have been many instances in my career where I have laid a lot on the line and made serious commitments to multiple investors and clients at the same time. I could have taken the easy way out and looked after myself. But I ended up taking the road less traveled, the one that required character, integrity, and accountability.

And in doing so, I can proudly say I made money for my clients first, which only benefited my own business later on.

As the late Colin Powell once said, "Once you break it, you own it!" That's how development projects and change-of-use projects work. It's money out, money out, and at times it feels like you're never going to see a return.

Don't fall prey to those fears. Any time I buy a property or sign onto a project, I commit to dragging it across the finish line. You just need to take it day by day; handle each task in the present while keeping your long-term vision and goals in mind.

The reason so many banks lend me money and so many different partners work with me is because I have built a track record of seeing projects through to the finish line, even if it means lesser profits for me. This is the most crucial client-engagement tactic you can ever master. Follow through on your deals, because your credibility is everything!

Train like a Professional Athlete

If you're a real estate agent, make it a priority to attend every single training opportunity that's available to you. I can't overstate this simple commandment enough. Doesn't matter if you've been in this business for a day or decades, training is the antidote to complacency.

Think of it this way: complacency is a career killer. Curiosity is a career builder.

So trust the process. Do everything in your power to remain engaged with professional training seminars and personal development courses.

To my mind it's one of the easiest and most beneficial things you can do to build a successful career. Just like a good pair of hockey skates, even the sharpest of skills need to be honed from time to time.

All you need to do is look at any high-performing athlete. Hockey. Football. Baseball. Soccer. Pick your favorite sport. Even after Wayne

Gretzky or LeBron James or Patrick Mahomes made it to the pinnacle of their sport, they kept training.

Training is what got them to the top of the mountain and what keeps them at the summit.

Gyms. Ice rinks. Batting cages. They're like second homes to professional athletes. All-stars are always dribbling, always trying to improve their stick handling, or fine-tuning their swings.

So why should we, in the real estate industry, view ourselves any differently? As I said at the start of this book, it's all about developing a proper mindset.

Do you want to be a lifelong learner or a short-term opportunist? The more you start blowing off sales meetings and avoiding real estate seminars, the greater the chance you're going to take shortcuts in other parts of your business.

If you don't have the time to listen to another real estate pro describe what's made them successful, what are the chances you're going to sit down with your clients and learn from them? Next thing you know, you're going to stop chasing down leads. You're going to fall off people's radars. And lose the pulse of your neighborhood.

I still, to this day, sign up for tons of training seminars and symposia. Truth be told it keeps me humble. Every time I sit down to listen to a real estate professional offer advice, I learn something new. Sometimes, it convinces me of things I shouldn't do; other times I'm introduced to strategies I need to start employing.

Either way it's a win-win for everyone involved. In any industry you either evolve or you die. It's that simple. You have to be coachable.

Nothing makes me groan more than listening to real estate agents who say, "I don't need training. I already know all that stuff already."

Really? Is your memory really that sharp? Nothing has ever slipped through the cracks? You've retained everything that's ever been presented to you? Instant and total recall, eh?

I don't buy it for a second. Peruse any of the latest research regarding the importance of repetition in the learning process, and it all points to pretty much the same findings. Repetitive learning hastens and strengthens the learning process.[12] In short, the more times you expose yourself to an idea, the greater the likelihood it's going to stick and become second nature.

So do as I do: go and sign up for a meeting about a topic you already feel you've mastered.

With Great Risk Comes Great Rewards

Top-rate salespeople are passionate about their work. I often use the phrase "fire in their belly" because I believe passion should be so palpable that you physically feel it coursing through your body.

Call it what you will. Nerves. Butterflies. Dithers. Your heart beating right through your chest. These are all good signs, in my opinion. Because when your body's physically shaking, that means you're putting something on the line. You've obviously mustered up enough courage to take on a new challenge or took on a new risk.

Think of it this way: luck and risk are both very real phenomena. You can control risk, but luck controls you. So stay focused on the things you can control. You can't control the flip of a coin, but you can control when you decide to flip it.

So stay focused on the bigger picture. I dreamed, for instance, of building a diversified portfolio of real estate business. I dreamed of helping everyday renters become homeowners. I dreamed of buying land and renovating buildings across greater Toronto.

---

12   Robert F. Bruner, "Repetition Is the First Principle of All Learning," ResearchGate, August 2001, https://www.researchgate.net/publication/228318502_Repetition_is_ the_First_Principle_of_All_Learning.

And it was precisely the scope of my ambitions that propelled me forward. It's the reason why I've developed millions of dollars in real estate projects over the course of my career. Every day I have the option of driving to eight different offices.

I don't rent any of them; I own them all because I refused to dream small dreams.

Here's the truth: plenty of people laughed at me, back in the 1990s, when I told them of my ambitions. So yes, people may laugh at you. Some will doubt you. And some will become so jealous, with every passing year, that they'll try their best to trip you up along the way.

You have to hold firm. Remember one of my other idiosyncratic phrases: "stick-to-itiveness." You have to hold your ground. Hold on to your dream. Be like Braveheart in the face of an oncoming English army. *Hold. Hold. Hold.* And you'll likely win the battle in the end.

You can't be afraid to take a risk, and your ability to leverage creative financing for your clients—and in return your own projects— is always your greatest asset. When you learn how to finance your clients, you become fearless when it comes to making deals happen for yourself. I have always leveraged my purchases and created equity in my purchases with very little money in the deal. I always took advantage of high-ratio financing, not subprime mortgaging or high-interest loans. For the most part, it's kept my clients and me out of trouble. I have also always worked with high-ratio government insurance or backed mortgages for my clients. Truthfully, I stay away from B lending—that is, funding from nontraditional lenders. It's been a principle that has proven to be the right strategy. You may need some high-interest financing to get into the deal; however, make it temporary with a take-out mortgage and looking at it as a short-term fix.

So yes, the skill sets and intangibles we've discussed matter. You need to be able to overcome rejection. Be persuasive. Get creative in terms of financing. Be a good communicator and even better listener. But you should know all that by now. The key is to go out in the world and dream the big dreams, the ones that no one else thinks are possible.

CHAPTER 10

CONCLUSION:

THE REAL WORLD OF REAL ESTATE

I'd like to close with one final story. It's a parable as much as a case study, which is as much about my journey as it is about the particular land in question.

The story began, back in 2009, during a period of absolute chaos for the real estate industry. The housing bubble had popped. The Great Recession had arrived.

It was not, as you might recall, the best time to be a real estate agent. Or a broker or developer or mortgage lender.

In every neighborhood foreclosure signs were appearing in front of homes. Underwater mortgages were rampant. Everyone and their brother was grousing about deflating property values.

The party, to put it bluntly, was over. No more balloons or confetti. Just a nasty hangover brought about by an irrational exuberance for an inflated market.

But here's the thing I've learned: in this business, you should fear the peaks a lot more than the valleys. If you need to reinvent yourself, better to do so during a downturn than a boom.

It just so happened that my wife and I, a year earlier, had decided it was time to make good on a long-percolating dream. At this point in our careers, we'd done just about everything you could do in the business—buy, sell, develop, renovate—except run our own brokerage.

Based on the abuses we'd seen ripple through the system, we'd agreed there was a little too much ego in our industry and not enough mentorship. So instead of going around and complaining about what was wrong inside the industry, we decided to actually do something about it.

We decided to open our own real estate office. We purchased our first Coldwell Banker franchise—The Real Estate Centre (TREC)—which we then molded in our own image and values.

We figured it would be refreshing to open an office that was gimmick-free. We'd make our mark the old-fashioned way—not by focusing on downlines and teams—but committing ourselves to the kinds of tried-and-true philosophies that never went out of style. White-glove service. Creative financing. Smart renovations. And above all a commitment to go the extra mile to help every potential client and real estate agent who walks in the front door.

Fortunately, given the 2009 downturn, we'd decided to build the practice slowly. We launched the business with a handful of employees in a newly renovated change-of-use building.

My new office represented just one of three parcels I'd acquired in the village of Maple, Ontario, which were all located in the vicinity of a newly constructed city hall for the city of Vaughan.

I saw the brokerage as a way to use my wealth-creation model to expand into other markets and then beyond Vaughan. An opportunity had presented itself for me to step into a bad situation in Newmarket. A broker had been terminated from being part of the Coldwell Banker family.

While all of this was unfolding, we attempted to retain some of the office's Realtors and convince them that we could rebuild the brand in Newmarket. We managed to retain seven Realtors and secured a crammed two-hundred-square-foot office. The cramped quarters didn't bother my wife and me one bit because we were energized by the prospect of building our business our way, from the ground up.

Then one day it happened. It was sort of like an epiphany, one of those moments when an idea embeds in your imagination and you know, deep down, that you're never going to be able to shake it loose.

While we continued to build our business, my attention was drawn to a pair of historic homes sitting on the corner of Davis Drive and Main Street in Newmarket. I must have passed that corner a thousand times over the years, but for some reason—in that moment, on that particular afternoon—I saw that corner lot with fresh eyes.

The property itself had been owned by the Robert Armstrong Real Estate Group, one of the first Coldwell Banker franchises in Canada, a brokerage that dated all the way back to the 1950s. The terminated brokerage I had just taken over was essentially the same brokerage that Robert Armstrong had started in this same location.

Ownership of the brokerage had changed hands a couple of times in the ensuing years, but those two historic buildings, rickety though they were, managed to survive.

Those two buildings boasted quite a history. In the early 1900s, they were known as the Union Hotel. But to accurately refer to the Union as a hotel was a bit of a stretch. It was, as every young man at the time knew, one of the most infamous brothels in greater Toronto.

Riffle through local historical records, and you'll find plenty of images of young ladies soliciting men from its second-floor balconies. As the area gentrified, the Union Hotel was sold off to what we might call more "respectable" parties.

After the Robert Armstrong group operated out of the building for many years, it had been expropriated by the region of York to build a new rapid transit system along Davis Drive where the building fronts onto.

As a result the region of York had to create a new site plan that preserved these two historical buildings yet created extra room for its new rapid transit system being built. The plan called for the lifting of these buildings off the ground, moving them to a temporary location, rebuilding new foundations in the new location minus the portion of the original lot required for the road widening, and then moving the buildings back onto the new foundation.

Although the municipality pulled out all the stops to preserve the buildings, all its hard work came with a cost. Once the region moved the two buildings back onto the new foundations in their original location, potential buyers had to agree to follow a new site plan and keep the two buildings intact. Needless to say the liquidation of the remaining lands and these two historical buildings made this parcel difficult to sell. In fact the historical designation actually devalued the land.

Suffice to say the amount of time and money spent to preserve these buildings was a sight to behold. The buildings, which had been designed by local architect John Ough, still contained many of the original moldings, woodwork, and staircases. All of which was carefully preserved during months of meticulous digging and work around the site.

Every couple of months or so, a developer would trot up the steps, thinking they might be the one to rescue these two grand old beauties from continued decay. And every single time, they'd leave disappointed.

Unsavable, they said. A money pit. Impossible. The cost required to restore those two buildings was a drag on the overall value of the land itself.

Suffice to say I saw things differently. Every time I stopped by the site, I began to renovate it in my mind's eye.

But I also knew I had to be patient. Sometimes, knowing what you want to do and knowing when to do it are two very different skills. So I did the prudent thing and waited. I made a point to stay in constant contact with the lawyers who represented the site as well as various appraisers and local officials.

My argument, every time I paid them a visit, came down to this: "There's no one in greater Toronto," I argued, "who is better equipped to save those buildings than I am."

By that time my wife and I had bought out the very same real estate brokerage, Robert Armstrong, that had owned those buildings in the 1950s. History, I figured, was on my side, but so was my experience. I wasn't just a real estate broker; I'd proven myself to be a successful real

> **Sometimes, knowing what you want to do and knowing when to do it are two very different skills.**

estate developer too—someone who'd already renovated an extraordinary number of historical buildings across greater Toronto.

I knew the pitfalls—not to mention the costs required—to show this site the care and attention it deserved. But most importantly of all, I told city officials that I knew exactly what to do with the land. I had a vision, clear as a four-K television, as to what needed to be done to preserve the site's historic character while modernizing it for the twenty-first century.

Originally, I'd played around with the idea of simply restoring the two buildings, but the more I studied the awful floor plans that I had to work with, the more I realized that a site plan amendment would be needed.

I not only preserved the front entrances of both structures as they currently stood, but I also created a common front entrance between the buildings as the main entrance. And then I made an impassioned argument to merge the two buildings in the back of both structures by constructing a massive addition that would act as a bridge between them.

It was my attempt, as I told officials, to preserve the character of the place while still modernizing it for contemporary use.

While everyone agreed that the buildings needed to be renovated, in some way, to meet modern building codes, I argued that the best way to do that was to build stairs and an elevator outside of the buildings. I also argued for the need to extend the height of the basements by jacking up the buildings at their foundation and removing a pillar that had been installed by the region, which essentially made the basements unusable. I replaced that old structural support with a 3,600-pound beam, which opened up the basement, creating a roomy space that boasted 10.6-foot ceilings.

I think local officials were surprised not only by my passion for the project but also by the sheer ambition of what I wanted to attempt.

The final piece of my pitch? I informed local officials that I was so smitten with this site that I planned to use it as one of my own real estate offices.

I knew that the wheels of change can turn achingly slowly, especially when it involves government-owned land. But I remained persistent in both my dreams and vision.

I kept in contact with city officials for more than five years, between 2013 and 2018. Every year I'd knock on someone else's door and ask if there were any developments on the Union Hotel space. And after every visit, I'd receive the same response. "Every single developer who looks at the buildings," they'd tell me, "is scared to death of that place. Everyone, it seems, but you, Dean."

So, every chance I got, I reminded them of my grand vision. Sometimes, I'd come bearing photographs, old and new, of other jobs I'd completed. Properties on Major Mackenzie Drive, our first office in the village of Maple, and one of my developments on Major Mackenzie Drive and Church Street in Richmond Hill.

I told them, at every single meeting, the same thing I've stressed in a dozen different places in a dozen different ways in this very book. Your biggest gains come when you make a commitment to transform something everyone else sees as worthless into something of long-standing value.

There are a lot of folks out there who will look at a site like that and say, "Yeah, there's potential there, but it's too much work for me to take on."

And it's precisely that kind of thinking that destroys neighborhoods. That motivates people to demolish good buildings. And most distressingly of all, motivates potentially talented real estate agents to quit our business.

I guess what I'm really trying to say is that the real estate business has taught me that there's no such thing as a perfect building—or perfect real estate agents. Most of us enter this business with flawed and damaged foundations. Maybe the paint work is a little chipped. Maybe the floor is a little uneven. And the windows don't exactly close all the way.

Doesn't matter to me in the least. Because to me everything's fixable, provided you put in the work necessary to get the job done. Doesn't matter where you might find yourself at the moment. New. Young. Old and experienced. Eager to grow.

If you devise a plan and can stick to it, chances are you'll make it to the other side.

But whatever you do, don't think small. Dream big. Be ambitious. Be willing to chase projects that other people tell you are impossible.

That's the real secret of real estate: it's seeing what no one else will see and then executing on your vision until it becomes a reality.

So yes, I did wind up convincing officials in York that I was the person best suited to save the Union Hotel. Even when other buyers tied it up and then walked away, I continued to tell officials that I was still their best bet.

I kept working on it. In my free time, I'd riffle through historical documents about the history of the buildings. I took the time to contact the previous owner's daughter, who supplied me with information that proved very useful in future negotiations with the municipality.

In short I played the long game.

And sure enough, in 2018, local officials called me and told me that they were now convinced I was, indeed, the best developer to save the site.

Although I originally tied it up for $1.3 million, I kept working to get a reduction. People told me I was crazy. "You'll never negotiate a reduction from a municipality," they told me. But I kept digging. I reached out to the architect York had hired to oversee the project. When he realized my enthusiasm for the project, he showed me a report that underscored the fragility of the bricks on the exterior of the buildings.

That tenacity—as well as that all-important report—convinced them to reduce the price. In 2020, after almost a decade of wrangling, I purchased the property for $1.1 million.

By this time my wife and I had greatly expanded our business. From a two-thousand-square-foot office with six or seven Realtors to eight offices with more than three hundred Realtors today, we'd built something out of nothing by ourselves—brick by brick. In 2022 TREC accomplished Number One Real Estate Brokerage in Canada for Coldwell Banker and sits among the top-tier brokerages across the entire Coldwell Banker network.

We expanded into other markets. We opened additional offices, all by doing something rather simple: we positioned ourselves as a client- and agent-first brokerage. It wasn't about our ego; it was about helping our agents become better Realtors.

Truth is we filled a void in the industry. No gimmicks, just mentorship. We teach our people everything we've learned. We don't keep secrets. We're committed, at this point in our careers, to sharing everything that we've learned with our people. We're committed to inspiring people not to pursue modest dreams, but rather to pursue the life-altering aspirations.

> **We filled a void in the industry. No gimmicks, just mentorship. We teach our people everything we've learned. We don't keep secrets.**

Which is the reason I wrote this book.

TREC has proven to be astoundingly successful because it's a reminder, to all who want to listen, that anyone can build a successful career by focusing on good old-fashioned white-glove service.

In the end that's what I hope this book will be for you: I hope it will be a reminder that with a little hard work and the right mindset, impossible dreams can be achieved.

I'm living proof of that fact. Every day I have the choice of driving to eight different offices across greater Toronto. My wife and I own most of them, which are all key facets of a bigger wealth-building vision, including what will be our ninth office in the Old Union Hotel in Newmarket.

It will be our crown jewel—a building that, at one time, no one wanted. Suffice to say it's now a building that everyone respects. In the end I hope our new office teaches just as much as it impresses. Hopefully it's a reminder of what to look for when you buy real estate.

A corner lot. Great location. Change of use. Unapologetically ambitious. Walking distance to public transportation and lots of shops. A model of new urbanism thinking. A building rooted in history but one that remains strikingly modern. A testament to the enduring power of constantly moving onward and upward.

Now that it's complete, our people will be able to collaborate with their peers in a shared workspace. There will be a coffee shop on site, called the Union, where clients and real estate agents alike can reenergize. But mostly I hope it will be an office that feels like home, a space that exemplifies the belief that everyone who works at The Real Estate Centre is part of an extended family that is committed to doing well for ourselves by doing good for others.

ACKNOWLEDGMENTS

I could not have achieved anything without my wife, Tania, and the drive that was amplified when our kids came into the bigger picture. The love and support of my wife have been an incredible source of motivation that has propelled me to achieve great things. But it wasn't until we had our children—David, Andrew, and Rachel Artenosi— that my drive for success was amplified to a whole new level. Knowing that I have family to provide for and set an example for has instilled in me an unwavering ambition to succeed. I am grateful every day for the inspiration they provide. Without their love and encouragement, I would not be where I am today.

To my entire TREC senior management team who have been my supporting cast in our growth and endeavors. Your dedication, intellectual advice, unwavering loyalty, hard work, and belief in our journey has been the foundation to our organization's success. Your positive attitude has been a pillar to our strength.

To Bob Lynch of Murray & Company and the late Jim Dysart from Peoples Trust and the BCI pension fund. You believed in my abilities when no one else would. You provided me with major construction loans and funding when I did not have the net worth. Your backing and belief in my creative deals elevated my skill set, which gave me the confidence to continue onward and upward to bigger deals.

To my father, Bruno; mother, Allida; brother, Daniel; and sister, Catherine. Your support for me as your son and brother has been unconditional. Through my journey I have gone through trying times both personally and professionally, and through it all, no matter the situation, you have always been there for me with emotional support and intellectual advice. My love for you is unconditional, and I draw on the strength of your support to persevere through my daily challenges and know you will always be there for me.

To my late father-in-law Girogio and mother-in-law Nella. Thank you for your support and for teaching me simplicity, staying grounded, exercising sound judgment, and the importance of supporting cast members through your journey. Your humility and "king maker" approach helped me through my journey more than you will ever know.

To all our Realtors at TREC, especially those that have been with us from the earlier years, thank you for believing in Tania and me and for leading by example. It is due to your leadership and loyalty that we have built the culture of an "agent-first brokerage," an "onward and upward" mindset, with the right focus to making a difference in your clients' lives and ultimately your own family lives. This is the safe place that we have provided our existing Realtors to be.

To the entire Coldwell Banker network, thank you for your leadership but most importantly for introducing us to your Ultimate Service system and culture. Through this unparalleled achievement and track record for service in the Canadian real estate industry, we have been able to create a mindset and culture for TREC sales representatives and elevate Realtor success to not only build a successful sales practice but also to incorporate this philosophy to real wealth creation through TREC's expertise in ownership, acquisition, and changing the use of real estate, thereby expanding our Realtors' skills sets.